FEAST OF FLAVOURS
from the Iranian Kitchen

FEAST OF **FLAVOURS**

from the

Iranian

Kitchen

A STEP-BY-STEP CULINARY ADVENTURE

Hayedeh Sedghi

Marshall Cavendish
Cuisine

Dedication

I would like to dedicate this book to my husband, Reza Kashkouli, without whose unfailing support and encouragement this book would not have been possible; and to my daughters, Sara and Saba, for being patient with me.

Photographer: Jambu Studio
Designer: Jailani Basari

Published by Marshall Cavendish Cuisine
An imprint of Marshall Cavendish International
1 New Industrial Road, Singapore 536196

Other Marshall Cavendish Offices:

Marshall Cavendish Ltd. 119 Wardour Street, London W1F 0UW, UK • Marshall Cavendish Corporation. 99 White Plains Road, Tarrytown NY 10591-9001, USA • Marshall Cavendish International (Thailand) Co Ltd. 253 Asoke, 12th Flr, Sukhumvit 21 Road, Klongtoey Nua, Wattana, Bangkok 10110, Thailand • Marshall Cavendish (Malaysia) Sdn Bhd, Times Subang, Lot 46, Subang Hi-Tech Industrial Park, Batu Tiga, 40000 Shah Alam, Selangor Darul Ehsan, Malaysia

Marshall Cavendish is a trademark of Times Publishing Limited

National Library Board Singapore Cataloguing in Publication Data

Sedghi, Hayedeh, 1969-
Feast of flavours from the Iranian kitchen : a step-by-step culinary adventure / Hayedeh Sedghi. –
Singapore : Marshall Cavendish Cuisine, c2007.
p. cm. – (Feast of flavours)
Includes index.
ISBN-13 : 978-981-261-281-6
ISBN-10 : 981-261-281-5

1. Cookery, Iranian. I. Title. II. Series: Feast of flavours

TX725.I7
641.5955 – dc22   SLS2006039604

Printed in Singapore by Times Graphics Pte Ltd

Introduction

Soups & Porridges

Vegetables & Salads

Seafood & Poultry

Meat

Rice

Desserts

Glossary & Index

COOKING TECHNIQUES

Iranian or Persian cooking can be done using simple cooking utensils, such as medium to large pots, stew and frying pans, wooden spoons, a masher, and so on. Nothing out of the ordinary, except for the flat kebab skewers that resemble long swords with no handles. Nevertheless, there are ways around them. The cooking techniques are similarly uncomplicated but require time and skills of assessment. Such skills traditionally come with experience gathered from daily practice, but this book aims to fast-track the learning process a little for its readers through the use of step-by-step photographs.

Because many of the country's dishes are characterised by slow-cooking, patience is a virtue in the Iranian kitchen. Be sure you have ample time, at least 2 hours, before deciding to prepare an Iranian meal—typically consisting of plain rice or a rice dish, a stew or two and a fresh salad, with yoghurt-based accompaniments and pickles often on the side. A soup is in order if serving only one stew, otherwise two stews are more common.

All recipes in this book make 4 servings if you follow the meal plan above. Otherwise, any of the rice dishes, excluding plain rice, will easily make a one-dish meal for 2–3 people. Although it takes 2–3 hours to prepare, an Iranian meal is worth every effort once it is placed on the table or *sofreh*—a large rectangular piece of embroidered cloth that traditional Iranians unfold and lay on the floor at mealtimes, and diners would sit along the two long sides after the spread of food has been placed along the centre.

Grilling (Broiling)

The technique of grilling skewered meat, whether lamb, beef or chicken, is an art form in Iran. Getting the beloved kebab right is no mean feat, from how the meat is lovingly kneaded and marinated to just how brightly the charcoal should glow before it is deemed worthy for the marinated meat, which will grace the grill for just long enough to cook through, remain deliciously juicy and become smokily charred in parts. In order for this to happen, the charcoal has to be very hot and glowing but with few flames. Iranian kebabs are also turned frequently as they cook and unlike other styles of barbecuing, a basting liquid is not often used.

Boiling and Simmering

Boiling is an important technique to master because rice is a primary staple in Iran and eaten every day. Rice, like pasta, should only be added to rapidly boiling water. Unlike pasta, however, Iranian cooks salt the water that soaks the rice rather than that in which the rice boils. Parboiled until half-cooked, the rice is then drained and put into another pot to dry out over low heat until fluffy.

The stew is the anchor of an Iranian meal. Slow-cooked to draw out the greatest amount of flavour from the ingredients used, Iranian stews typically feature a type of red meat, which could be lamb or beef; a mixture of fresh or dried herbs; vegetables such as the much-loved aubergines (eggplants/brinjals), carrots and potatoes; and pulses such as kidney beans or split peas. Stews should be always simmered, that means keeping the liquid at a low boil or barely over the boiling point. The gentle movement of the liquid and its consistent temperature ensure that the solid ingredients being stewed keep their shape and become tender, not hard, with prolonged cooking. Cooked in this way, each stew takes about 2 hours to prepare, but with some planning, two or more stews can be simmering concurrently.

Pan- and Shallow-frying

Pan- and shallow-frying are far more common in the Iranian kitchen than deep-frying. In Iranian cooking, pan-frying is a quick cooking method that is used to prepare certain ingredients for their inclusion in the main dish. Shallow-frying, on the other hand, is more often used for preparing light meals, such as Potato and Meat Cutlets (*Kotlet*). The key difference between the two methods is the amount of oil used. When pan-frying, the oil used is just enough to coat the frying surface of the pan in a thin layer, while shallow-frying means that the oil used should immerse the fried items about halfway or slightly less. Avoid overcrowding the pan when shallow-frying because it causes the temperature of the oil to drop suddenly, and when that happens, the fried items will absorb more oil and become soggy.

Baking

The oven is rarely used in the Iranian kitchen, but when it is, it is usually for one of two reasons: first, when charcoal grilling is not an option; and second, when a dish needs to be kept warm at low heat for its flavours to develop and mature. The Baked Aubergine Dip and Minced Lamb Kebab (*Kabab-e Koobideh*) recipes in this book are examples of how the oven is utilised when charcoal heat is unavailable. While there is far less cleaning up to do when the oven is used, the smoky flavour of the original dish is also sacrificed. Fried Aubergine Stew (*Khoresh-e Bademjan*) illustrates the second point. Because the aubergines and meat are cooked separately, the combined dish is placed in the oven at very low heat so their flavours can interact and mature.

Pickling

Harking back to the days before refrigeration was available, Iranian cooks made pickles out of various ingredients to preserve them for the colder months. Usually served on the side in small bowls, pickles are eaten for a contrast of flavours and to whet the appetite, much like chutneys and relish. Sometimes, pickles are incorporated into a dish, such as Chicken Mayonnaise Salad (*Salad Olvieh*), for example. While some cooks today still take pride in making their own, most others have taken to buying ready-made ones from delicatessen-like shops or supermarkets. The tray below contains (*clockwise from top*) pickled Persian cucumbers, spicy mixed vegetable relish, non-spicy mixed vegetable relish, pickled sour cherries, and whole heads of pickled garlic in the centre.

COOKING UTENSILS

Wooden Spoons

These spoons are favoured by Iranian cooks primarily because of the frequent, and sometimes constant, stirring required by many slow-simmered stews and favourite desserts such as rice puddings. Given how popular non-stick pots and pans are in Iran and Iranian kitchens around the world, wooden spoons, like plastic ones, are common because they can be used on non-stick surfaces without causing scratches. Unlike plastic, however, wood has the added advantage of being able to withstand prolonged heat without warping.

Knives

Iranian cooks rely mostly on a vegetable knife (*right*) in the kitchen. In fact, many do not even use a chopping board, with most of the slicing and dicing done over the pot. The carving knife (*left*) is occasionally used to fillet whole fish or cut larger, tougher cuts of meat.

Colander

The colander is something that Iranian cooks are bound to use several times a day, from washing uncooked rice and draining parboiled rice to washing and draining different fresh herbs and pulses for any of a variety of stews. Typically bowl-shaped with many holes to facilitate the draining away of liquid, the colander can be made of plastic or metal. It may be useful to have several colanders of different sizes when preparing an Iranian meal.

Non-stick Pots and Pans

The advent of non-stick cooking utensils was probably the single most important development in Iranian cooking. They not only saved much time and labour when it came to cleaning, but also made certain difficult dishes, such as *Tah Chin-e Morgh* (Rice Cooked with Yoghurt and Chicken) or the well-loved *tadig* (see pg 82) much easier to achieve. With non-stick pots, even novice cooks can turn out thick barley soup or gummy rice puddings with confidence and crisp-edged rice dishes using far less oil.

Grater

Although the grater is not essential for Iranian cooking, it does lighten the load of the cook when it comes to repetitive chopping and slicing. Dishes that require lots of minced, julienned or thinly sliced ingredients are made that much easier with the grater.

Flat Skewers

The Iranian love for a good *chelo kabab* —minced lamb kebab served on a bed of fluffy rice with a knob of butter, char-grilled tomatoes, a handful of fresh basil leaves and shakers of salt and sumac on the side—is impossible to ignore. To make minced lamb kebab, one would need these flat skewers, which are about 60 cm (24 in) in length and range from 1.5 cm ($^3/_4$ in) to 3 cm ($1^1/_2$ in) wide. The minced meat is shaped and pressed onto them so that it can later be frequently turned over intense charcoal heat to cook. This is one type of kebab that cannot be prepared using regular rod skewers, and such flat skewers are hard to find outside of Iran. Nevertheless, minced lamb kebabs can be made at home by shaping the meat into strips on a baking tray and then baking them in the oven, although the smoky, char-grilled flavour will be sacrificed.

Flame Tamer

This is one item that would be present in most Iranian kitchens, but is not truly essential to Iranian cooking. Flame tamers today come in various shapes and sizes. The traditional and most commonly seen one is a round metal disc that is perforated with holes and has a handle. The flame tamer's purpose, as its name suggests, is to diffuse heat. Although it is popular, it does not affect the overall dish dramatically. Simply use lower heat if without a flame tamer.

Masher

The Iranian version of a masher looks faintly like a plunger and is about 30 cm (12 in) in length. Unlike western mashers, which may have a grid pattern, be perforated with holes or have connected parallel rods at one end, the Iranian masher has a solid base. Apart from using it to mash ingredients such as boiled potatoes during the preparation of a dish, Iranian cooks also use this masher to serve *abgoosht* or *dizi* dishes, which are stews of meat, pulses and vegetables served in the form of a thick paste; the solid ingredients of the stew are drained from the gravy and mashed into a paste that is eaten with bread. The gravy is served separately and drunk like a soup with some bread torn into little pieces.

Oil Spoon

Possibly unique to the Iranian kitchen, this metal spoon has a few holes that are meant to facilitate the drizzling of oil or melted butter over cooked rice dishes just before serving. Iranians traditionally serve their rice dishes piled high on serving platters, and to use this spoon, one would hold it above the rice in one hand and the amount of oil or butter to be drizzled over in the other. As the oil or butter is poured onto the spoon, the hand holding the metal spoon would move in a circular motion to ensure even distribution all over the rice.

Rice Serving Spoon

This is a traditional rice serving spoon. Typically, it would be placed on the side of a large plate or serving platter of rice for diners to use to pile fluffy rice onto their own plates. The smooth side of the scoop is where one would dig into the rice. As these spoons endure some wear and tear and are no longer ideal for the dinner table or *sofreh*, they can double up as large metal spoons similar to those used in Western cooking, only the scoop is shallower. When the serving spoon becomes a kitchen utensil, it is especially useful for spooning parboiled rice into a pot to dry out over low heat.

Teapot

Tea drinking is so central to the Iranian way of life that it is impossible for any family to be without a teapot (*above*) or samovar of some kind. Iranian teacups are similar to others in the region, in that they are small and clear, with no handle but commonly with some gilt decoration. To use the teapot shown, quarter-fill the teapot with dried tea leaves, then add hot water and cover. Light a tea candle and place it inside the stand, then place the teapot on top. Allow to steep for 5–10 minutes and a tea concentrate is made. To serve, pour a small quantity of the tea concentrate into each teacup (it should be between one-quarter and one-third full), then add hot water until it is three-quarters full; the tea should be a deep ruby red in colour and clear.

Caviar Bowl

Usually made of a brass- or copper-based material and ornately decorated, the bowl on three legs with a dome-shaped cover (*right*) is what Iranians traditionally use to serve caviar. The history of caviar in Iran is centuries-long and illustrious, with the Caspian Sea in the country's north producing several varieties of superior and internationally sought-after caviar. Today, however, the sturgeon population has dwindled to near-extinction levels and there is international pressure to stop illegal fishing of wild sturgeons by Iran's neighbours. Within Iran, the caviar industry is controlled by the government and a research centre dedicated to sturgeons in the Caspian Sea has made encouraging advances in sturgeon farming.

WEIGHTS & MEASURES

Quantities for this book are given in Metric and American (spoon and cup) measures. Standard spoon and cup measurements used are: 1 teaspoon = 5 ml, 1 dessertspoon = 10 ml, 1 tablespoon = 15 ml, 1 cup = 250 ml. All measures are level unless otherwise stated.

LIQUID AND VOLUME MEASURES

Metric	Imperial	American
5 ml	$1/6$ fl oz	1 teaspoon
10 ml	$1/3$ fl oz	1 dessertspoon
15 ml	$1/2$ fl oz	1 tablespoon
60 ml	2 fl oz	$1/4$ cup (4 tablespoons)
85 ml	$2^1/2$ fl oz	$1/3$ cup
90 ml	3 fl oz	$3/8$ cup (6 tablespoons)
125 ml	4 fl oz	$1/2$ cup
180 ml	6 fl oz	$3/4$ cup
250 ml	8 fl oz	1 cup
300 ml	10 fl oz ($1/2$ pint)	$1^1/4$ cup
375 ml	12 fl oz	$1^1/2$ cup
435 ml	14 fl oz	$1^3/4$ cup
500 ml	16 fl oz	2 cups
625 ml	20 fl oz (1 pint)	$2^1/2$ cups
750 ml	24 fl oz ($1^1/5$ pint)	3 cups
1 litre	32 fl oz ($1^3/5$ pint)	4 cups
1.25 litres	40 fl oz (2 pints)	5 cups
1.5 litres	48 fl oz ($2^2/5$ pints)	6 cups
2.5 litres	80 fl oz (4 pints)	10 cups

DRY MEASURES

Metric	Imperial
30 g	1 oz
45 g	$1^1/2$ oz
55 g	2 oz
70 g	$2^1/2$ oz
85 g	3 oz
100 g	$3^1/2$ oz
110 g	4 oz
125 g	$4^1/2$ oz
140 g	5 oz
280 g	10 oz
450 g	16 oz (1 lb)
500 g	1 lb, $1^1/2$ oz
700 g	$1^1/2$ lb
800 g	$1^3/4$ lb
1 kg	2 lb, 3 oz
1.5 kg	3 lb, $4^1/2$ oz
2 kg	4 lb, 6 oz

LENGTH

Metric	Imperial
0.5 cm	$1/4$ in
1 cm	$1/2$ in
1.5 cm	$3/4$ in
2.5 cm	1 in

OVEN TEMPERATURE

	°C	°F	Gas Regulo
Very slow	120	250	1
Slow	150	300	2
Moderately slow	160	325	3
Moderate	180	350	4
Moderately hot	190/200	370/400	5/6
Hot	210/220	410/440	6/7
Very hot	230	450	8
Super hot	250/290	475/550	9/10

ABBREVIATION

Tbsp	tablespoon
tsp	teaspoon
kg	kilogram
g	gram
l	litres
ml	millilitres

Dried chickpeas take a tremendously long time to become tender when cooking. Pre-soaking them helps to shorten the cooking time.

Frying the dried mint leaves in oil not only makes them aromatic, but also infuses the oil with a unique herby flavour. Double or treble the amount of mint used, if desired.

If whey is unavailable, garnish with cream instead, but do not replace whey in this recipe with cream—the result will be disasterous!

Tip: For prettier presentation, toss onion slices for garnishing in a saffron solution—2 tsp ground saffron stirred in 2 Tbsp hot water—before frying so they take on a rich orangy-red colour.

Step-By-Step

TRADITIONAL NOODLE SOUP *(ASH-E RESHTEH)*

This soup is thick with ingredients, flavour and goodness. It was traditionally prepared to mark the passing of winter into spring.

Ingredients

Dried kidney beans	90 g (3 oz / $\frac{1}{2}$ cup), soaked in water for 2–3 hours and drained
Dried chickpeas	100 g (3$\frac{1}{2}$ oz / $\frac{1}{2}$ cup), soaked in water for 2–3 hours and drained
Cooking oil	2 Tbsp
Onion	1, large, peeled and finely diced
French (Puy) lentils	100 g (3$\frac{1}{2}$ oz / $\frac{1}{2}$ cup)
Reshteh (Iranian dried wheat noodles) or *kishimen* (flat Japanese wheat noodles)	200 g (7 oz)
Salt	to taste
Ground black pepper	to taste
Whey (optional)	250–500 ml (8–16 fl oz / 1–2 cups), depending on taste

Greens

Chinese chives	100 g (3$\frac{1}{2}$ oz)
Coriander leaves (cilantro)	100 g (3$\frac{1}{2}$ oz)
Chinese celery	100 g (3$\frac{1}{2}$ oz)
Dill	100 g (3$\frac{1}{2}$ oz)
Spinach	150 g (5$\frac{1}{3}$ oz)

Garnishing

Cooking oil	4 Tbsp
Onion	1, peeled and thinly sliced
Dried mint leaves	1 Tbsp or more to taste
Cream (optional)	

Method

- Wash and drain greens well, then finely chop them together and set aside.
- Put kidney beans and chickpeas in a pot. Add 2 litres (64 fl oz / 8 cups) water and simmer for about 1$\frac{1}{2}$ hours or until pulses are tender. If pot dries up while pulses are simmering and they are still hard, add some hot water and continue simmering until they are tender; repeat, if necessary.
- Heat 2 Tbsp oil in a large, clean pot and fry onion over medium-low heat until translucent and lightly browned.
- Add chopped greens and fry for 1–2 minutes or until they are aromatic.

- Add cooked pulses and their cooking liquid, then lentils. Simmer until lentils soften, about 20 minutes.
- Add noodles and gently stir through to mix well with other ingredients, then simmer until they soften. Avoid frequent stirring as it causes the noodles to break.
- Just before serving, season to taste with salt and pepper. If using whey, add desired amount now, reserving some for garnishing, and stir through. Keep warm.
- Prepare garnishing. Heat 2 Tbsp oil in a pan and fry onion until golden and aromatic, then drain and set aside.

- Heat remaining oil in a clean pan and lightly fry dried mint leaves for 1 minute or until aromatic, then remove from heat.
- To serve, ladle soup into a serving bowl and garnish as desired with cream, if not using whey, fried mint leaves and fried onion slices.

MIXED HERB PORRIDGE
(ASH-E SHOLLEH GHALAM KAR)

Deeply aromatic and appetising from a rich mixture of herbs, this porridge is so thick and nutritious, it could easily be a meal in itself.

Ingredients

Cooking oil	2 Tbsp
Onion	1, large, peeled and finely diced
Lamb or beef	300 g (10 oz), cut into small chunks
Ground turmeric	1 tsp
Dried kidney beans	90 g (3 oz / $^1/_2$ cup), soaked in water for 2–3 hours and drained
Dried chickpeas	100 g (3$^1/_2$ oz / $^1/_2$ cup), soaked in water for 2–3 hours and drained
Thai fragrant rice	75 g (2$^1/_2$ oz), soaked in water for 30 minutes and drained
French (Puy) lentils	100 g (3$^1/_2$ oz / $^1/_2$ cup)
Salt	to taste
Ground black pepper	to taste

Greens

Chinese chives	100 g (3$^1/_2$ oz)
Coriander leaves (cilantro)	100 g (3$^1/_2$ oz)
Chinese celery	100 g (3$^1/_2$ oz)
Dill	100 g (3$^1/_2$ oz)
Spinach	100 g (3$^1/_2$ oz)

Garnishing (optional)

Cooking oil	2 Tbsp
Onion	1, peeled and thinly sliced

Step-By-Step

Soaking the dried kidney beans in water for at least 2 hours before cooking shortens the cooking time. The same goes for dried chickpeas.

Wash rice well, then soak in water for 30 minutes and drain before cooking. This, too, helps to shorten cooking time.

Wash and drain herbs, then finely chop them together. This could be done in a blender (processor) to save time, but much of the herb juices will also be lost.

Method

- Wash greens thoroughly and drain well, then finely chop them together and set aside.
- Heat 2 Tbsp oil in a large pot and fry onion over medium-low heat until translucent and lightly browned.
- Add meat and turmeric and fry until meat changes colour.

- Add beans, chickpeas and 2 litres (64 fl oz / 8 cups) water. Simmer until pulses are tender, about 1$^1/_2$ hours.
- Add rice, lentils and greens. Continue simmering, stirring occasionally to prevent ingredients at the bottom from burning, until lentils are tender.
- Season to taste with salt and pepper just before serving and keep warm.

- Prepare garnishing, if using. Heat 2 Tbsp oil in a clean pan and fry sliced onion until golden brown and aromatic.
- To serve, ladle soup into a serving bowl and top with fried onion, if using.

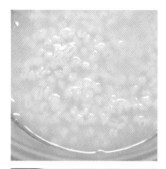

Simmer barley in 1.25 litres (40 fl oz / 5 cups) water until the grains are fluffy and tender, and the water is cloudy. This takes about 45 minutes.

Leave chicken to cool completely in the cooking liquid before draining to shred. This makes the chicken more flavourful.

Depending on your preference, stir in double (heavy) cream or milk just before serving. Cream is the tastier choice, while milk is the more health-conscious one.

S t e p - B y - S t e p

BARLEY SOUP *(SOOP-E JO)*

The buttery smooth and creamy texture of this nutritious soup makes it enticing and heartwarming.

Ingredients

Barley	110 g (4 oz / ½ cup), washed and soaked in water for at least 2 hours, then drained
Chicken breast meat	150 g (5⅓ oz), cut into long strips
Onion	1, small, peeled and finely diced
Carrot	1, medium, peeled if desired and grated
Chicken stock cubes	2, or 4 tsp, if using granules
Butter	2 Tbsp
Double (heavy) cream or milk	250 ml (8 fl oz / 1 cup)
Salt	to taste
Ground black pepper	to taste
Lime juice (optional)	2 Tbsp
Chinese celery	50 g (2 oz), chopped

Method

- Put barley in a pot. Add 1.25 litres (40 fl oz / 5 cups) water and simmer over low heat until the grains soften, about 45 minutes. Stir frequently to prevent sticking.
- Meanwhile, put chicken and onion in a small pot. Add 250 ml (8 fl oz / 1 cup) water and cook over low heat for about 15 minutes or until chicken is cooked. Remove from heat and allow to cool.
- Drain cooled chicken and shred. When barley grains are fluffy and tender, add chicken and stir through.

- Add carrot, stock cubes and butter. Continue to cook over low heat for about 40 minutes or until very thick.
- Just before serving, stir in cream or milk and season to taste with salt and pepper. Add lime juice, if using.
- To serve, ladle into a soup tureen or individual serving bowls and garnish with Chinese celery. Add an extra sprinkling of pepper, if desired.
- This recipe can be prepared with a slow cooker, but it will take about 3 hours. To quicken this process slightly, parboil pre-soaked barley over stove-top heat first.

OATMEAL PORRIDGE *(HALIM)*

This porridge is traditionally prepared with wheat grains, which take several hours longer to cook. Quick-cooking oatmeal shortens cooking time considerably without seriously compromising taste.

Ingredients

Beef or lamb	150 g (5 oz), cut into egg-size chunks
Onion	1, medium, peeled and cut into chunks
Salt	1 tsp
Quick-cooking oatmeal	85 g (3 oz / 1 cup)
Butter	2 Tbsp
Ground cinnamon	to taste
Sugar (optional)	to taste

Step-By-Step

Quick-cooking oatmeal in this recipe can be replaced with 100 g (3½ oz) rolled oats for a chewier texture, if preferred, but cooking time will lengthen.

After meat pieces have cooled in their cooking liquid, drain and shred or pound for a smoother porridge texture.

If a more robust flavour is preferred, pour meat cooking liquid into a measuring cup and add water to make 1 litre (32 fl oz / 4 cups), then use it to cook oatmeal.

Method

- Place meat, onion and salt in a pot. Pour in 750 ml (24 fl oz / 3 cups) water and cook over low heat until meat is tender, about 1 hour. Remove from heat and allow to cool.
- Drain cooled meat and shred or pound until fine. Set aside.

- Place oatmeal in a pot and add 1 litre (32 fl oz / 4 cups) water. Bring to the boil over low heat, stirring constantly.
- Add meat and continue to simmer, still stirring constantly, for 30 minutes or until porridge is thickened.
- Just before serving, add butter and stir until it is totally melted, then remove from heat.

- To serve, ladle porridge into a large serving bowl or individual ones and sprinkle cinnamon over. Serve porridge with sugar on the side, if using, for diners to add as they desire.

Spinach in Yoghurt (*Borani Esfenaj*)

Cucumber, Onion and Yoghurt Dip (*Mast-o Khiar*)

Cucumber, Onion and Tomato Salad, Shiraz Style (*Salad-e Shirazi*)

Mixed Herb Cutlets (*Kookoo Sabzi*)

Baked Aubergine Dip

Baked Aubergines with Garlic and Egg (*Mirza Ghasemi*)

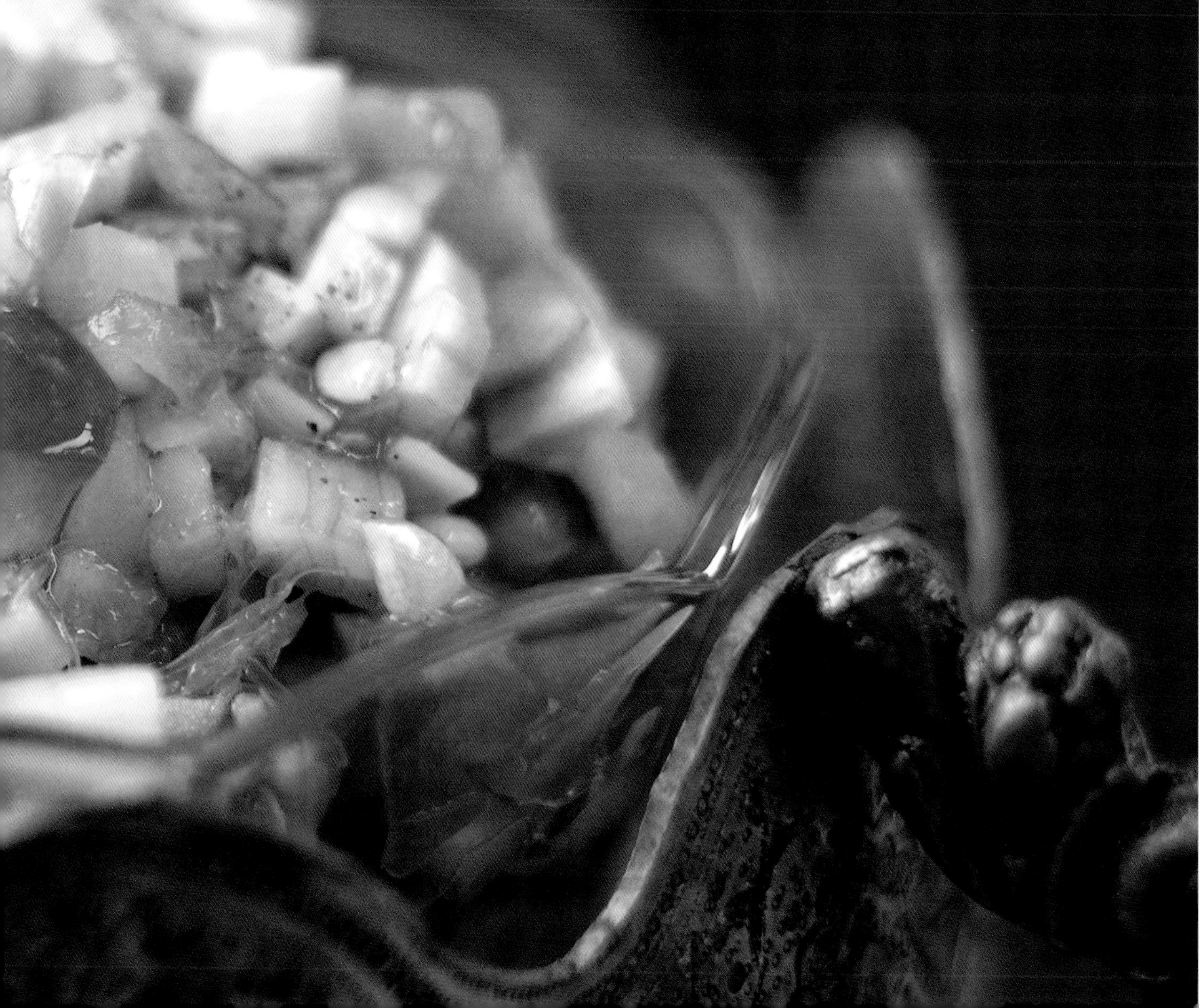

VEGETABLES & SALADS

Spinach can be cooked a day ahead and stored in the refrigerator, covered. More liquid emerges overnight, so drain spinach well before use.

With squeezed spinach in a mixing bowl, grate garlic over in long shreds before adding yoghurt and mixing well.

Step-By-Step

SPINACH IN YOGHURT
(BORANI ESFENAJ)

The distinct flavours of spinach and raw garlic mesh beautifully with slightly tangy yoghurt to form an appetising dip or side dish.

Ingredients

Spinach	400 g (13$\frac{1}{2}$ oz), trimmed and cut into 3-cm (1$\frac{1}{2}$-in) lengths
Garlic	2 cloves, peeled and finely grated
Plain or Greek yoghurt	500 ml (16 fl oz / 2 cups)
Salt	to taste
Ground black pepper	to taste

Method

- Wash and drain spinach, then transfer to a non-stick pot. Place pot over very low heat and stir spinach around to prevent sticking until it collapses and cooks in its own liquid. Alternatively, steam cleaned spinach for 15 minutes or until cooked.
- Drain cooked spinach well and squeeze out excess liquid. Spinach should be moist to the touch, but not dripping wet.

- Put spinach into a mixing bowl. Grate garlic over, then add yoghurt and mix well. Season mixture to taste with salt and pepper.
- Garnish, if desired, with dried roses or drizzle with saffron solution: stir 1 tsp ground saffron in 1 Tbsp hot water and allow to cool.

- Serve as a dip with flat bread or chips for a light appetiser or as an accompaniment to the main meal.

CUCUMBER, ONION AND YOGHURT DIP

(MAST-O KHIAR)

Recipes for this raita-like dip vary slightly throughout the country. This one has been pared down to its most basic, so be creative and add such ingredients as button mushrooms, ginger, garlic and walnuts to make it your own.

Ingredients

Japanese cucumbers	3, ends trimmed
Onion	1, medium, peeled
Plain or Greek yoghurt	500 ml (16 fl oz / 2 cups)
Salt	to taste
Ground black pepper	to taste

Step-By-Step

If Japanese cucumbers are unavailable, use 2 medium-size, regular cucumbers. Trim off each end, remove pulpy cores and peel, if desired, before dicing.

If preferred, grate onion and cucumbers into shreds instead of dicing (as pictured), but squeeze out excess liquid from grated cucumbers before adding yoghurt.

Method

- Trim off both ends of each cucumber and peel, if desired. Finely dice cucumbers and place in a mixing bowl.
- Finely dice onion and add to cucumbers, then mix in yoghurt. Season to taste with salt and pepper.
- Garnish, if desired, with a sprinkling of dried mint leaves.
- Serve as a pre-meal dip or an accompaniment to the main meal.

CUCUMBER, ONION AND TOMATO SALAD, SHIRAZ STYLE *(SALAD-E SHIRAZI)*

This zesty and refreshing salad originated from Shiraz, where it varies from household to household because people have adapted it to include seasonal ingredients and to suit their own tastes. Feel free to add other ingredients such as green capsicum (bell pepper) for variation.

Ingredients

Japanese cucumbers	3, or 2 medium-size regular cucumbers
Tomatoes	2, medium
Onion	1, medium, peeled

Dressing (combined)

Lime juice	4 Tbsp
Olive oil	1 Tbsp
Salt	to taste
Ground black pepper (optional)	to taste

S t e p - B y - S t e p

Finely dice trimmed cucumbers, tomatoes and peeled onion.

Salad can be prepared up until this stage—mixed but not dressed—and refrigerated, covered, for a few hours until it is needed.

Prepare dressing by stirring together lime juice and olive oil, then season to taste with salt and pepper, if using. Some cooks are also known to add a sprinkling of dried mint.

Method

- Trim off both ends of each cucumber and peel, if desired. Finely dice cucumbers and set aside. If using regular cucumbers, trim off each end, remove pulpy cores and peel, if desired, before dicing.
- Finely dice tomatoes and onion, then toss together with cucumbers until well-mixed.
- Transfer mixed vegetables to a serving bowl and refrigerate, covered, if not serving immediately.
- Just before serving, prepare dressing to pour over salad and toss to mix.

If using dried herbs, mix them together and soak mixture in some water to rehydrate before draining when needed.

Crack eggs into a mixing bowl and beat lightly, then add herbs; barberries, if using; flour; and salt and pepper to taste. Mix well.

After cooking over low heat for 10 minutes, cut herb pancake into wedge slices while it is still in the pan and turn each one over to brown the other side.

Tip: Instead of pan-frying, pour herb mixture into an ovenproof container similar in volume size to the pan and bake in a preheated oven at 180°C (350°F) for 30 minutes or until cooked through.

S t e p - B y - S t e p

MIXED HERB CUTLETS
(KOOKOO SABZI)

Crisp-edged and deeply aromatic, this dish is typically prepared for a quick, light meal and is part of everyday family fare. It has no place at a formal meal or one involving guests.

Ingredients

Eggs	3, large
Crushed walnuts	1 Tbsp
Dried barberries (optional)	1 Tbsp
Plain (all-purpose) flour	1 Tbsp
Salt	to taste
Ground black pepper	to taste
Cooking oil	4 Tbsp + as required

Herbs

Chinese celery	150 g (5$^1/_3$ oz), or 40 g (1$^1/_4$ oz) dried
Chinese chives	150 g (5$^1/_3$ oz), or 40 g (1$^1/_4$ oz) dried
Dill	150 g (5$^1/_3$ oz), or 40 g (1$^1/_4$ oz) dried
Coriander leaves (cilantro)	150 g (5$^1/_3$ oz), or 40 g (1$^1/_4$ oz) dried

Method

- Wash and drain fresh herbs well, then finely chop them together.
- Crack eggs into a mixing bowl and beat lightly. Add herbs and all remaining ingredients, except oil, and mix well.
- Heat 4 Tbsp oil in a 20-cm (8-in) round frying pan (skillet). Add herb mixture and spread it out evenly.
- Cover pan and cook over low heat for 10 minutes or until underside is set and lightly browned. Add a little more oil, if necessary, to prevent sticking.
- Cut herb pancake into wedge slices while it is still in the pan, then turn each slice over to lightly brown the other side.
- Dish out to a plate and serve warm.

BAKED AUBERGINE DIP

A favourite vegetable of most Persian Iranians, the aubergine is featured most famously in *Khoresh-e Bademjan* (Fried Aubergine Stew). Pre-meal, appetiser dips prepared with aubergines are not uncommon in the Middle East, with Arab, Turkish and Lebanese versions.

Ingredients

Aubergines (eggplants/brinjals)	2 large, or 3 medium
Garlic	2 large cloves, peeled and grated
Plain or Greek yoghurt	500 ml (16 fl oz / 2 cups)
Salt	to taste
Ground black pepper	to taste

Step-By-Step

An alternative to oven-baking the aubergines (as pictured) is to grill (broil) them over hot charcoal until similarly softened. This gives them a lovely smoky flavour.

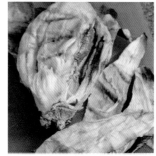

Peel cooked aubergines when they have cooled. Their skins should come off easily.

Roughly chop the softened flesh of the cooked aubergines and place in a bowl before mixing in other ingredients.

Method

- Bake aubergines in a preheated oven at 200°C (400°F) for about 30 minutes or until flesh is fully softened, turning over halfway. Remove and allow to cool.
- Peel cooled aubergines and roughly chop softened flesh, then put into a mixing bowl.
- Add garlic and yoghurt and mix well, then season to taste with salt and pepper.
- If not serving immediately, cover and refrigerate until needed. In fact, preparing this dip 2–3 hours before it is served allows the flavours to develop and mature.

Place cleaned aubergines whole into the oven, preheated at 200°C (400°F), and bake for 30 minutes, turning over halfway, until flesh inside is softened.

To make tomato easier to peel, blanch it in hot water for about 30 seconds. Some cooks transfer the tomato from hot to cold water to further separate the skin.

After adding tomato and aubergines, continue to sauté over medium-low heat until their juices have evaporated.

BAKED AUBERGINES WITH GARLIC AND EGG
(MIRZA GHASEMI)

The mushy texture of cooked aubergines, flavoured by robust garlic and tangy tomato, makes this a delicious savoury bread spread. This dish is mostly served in between mealtimes.

Ingredients

Aubergines (eggplants/brinjals)	2 large, or 3 medium, washed and dried
Tomato	1, large
Cooking oil	2 Tbsp
Garlic	5–6 large cloves, peeled and coarsely chopped
Eggs	3, medium
Salt	to taste
Ground black pepper	to taste

Method

- Bake aubergines in a preheated oven at 200°C (400°F) for about 30 minutes or until flesh is fully softened, turning over halfway. Remove and allow to cool.
- Meanwhile, blanch tomato in hot water for about 30 seconds or until skin separates. Peel tomato, then finely dice and set aside.

- Peel cooled aubergines and roughly chop softened flesh. Set aside.
- Heat oil in a large pan and fry garlic over medium-low heat until fragrant.
- Add tomato and aubergines. Fry them together until their juices have evaporated and mixture is quite dry.

- Push mixture to one side of pan and crack eggs where pan is empty. Cook eggs, stirring, until they are scrambled, then mix all ingredients together.
- Season to taste with salt and pepper before dishing out to serve.
- Some Iranian cooks are known to top this cooked mixture with an egg, fried sunny-side up.

SEAFOOD & POULTRY

Do not doubt the large quantity of coriander (cilantro) called for in this recipe as the leaves collapse and reduce considerably with sautéing.

Heat a greased pan and fry seasoned fish on both sides until lightly golden. Do not overcrowd pan and re-grease as necessary.

After adding fried fish steaks to sautéed herbs, refrain from frequent or vigorous stirring to prevent them from breaking up or flaking.

HERBED FISH STEW
(KHORESH-E GHALIEH MAHI)

This stew—fish steaks bathed in a richly herb-infused liquid and slow-simmered until fork-tender—is irresistibly aromatic and delicious. For variation, prepare this dish with prawns (shrimps) instead of fish.

Ingredients

Coriander leaves (cilantro)	600 g (1 lb 5 oz)
Fenugreek leaves (*methi*)	100 g (3¹/₂ oz), or 25 g (1 oz) dried
Firm fish steaks	8, total about 1.2 kg (2 lb 8 oz), use Spanish mackerel or similar
Salt	to taste
Cooking oil	2 Tbsp + as required
Onion	1, large, peeled and finely diced
Garlic	1 head, peeled and finely chopped
Ground turmeric	1 tsp
Fish curry powder	1 Tbsp
Chilli powder	to taste
Tamarind pulp	250 g (9 oz), mixed with 500 ml (16 fl oz / 2 cups) water and strained for juice

Method

- Trim off roots and tough lower stems of coriander and discard. Wash and drain remainder well, then chop finely and set aside. Repeat with fenugreek, if using fresh leaves.
- Season fish steaks with salt and pan-fry in oil on both sides until lightly golden, then remove and drain on paper towels. Re-oil pan as necessary.

- Heat 2 Tbsp oil in a pot and fry onion over medium-low heat until translucent and lightly browned. Add garlic, turmeric and curry and chilli powders. Stir to mix.
- Add fenugreek and fry until aromatic, then add coriander and continue to fry, stirring constantly, for 8–10 minutes or until coriander collapses and darkens.

- Add fried fish, tamarind juice and salt to taste, then pour in 750 ml (24 fl oz / 3 cups) water and cook over low heat for 1 hour or until liquid is reduced to about 250 ml (8 fl oz / 1 cup) and thick. Adjust seasoning to taste, if necessary.
- Serve warm with plain rice (see pg 82).

FRIED HERB-STUFFED FISH
(MAHI SHEKAM GEREFTEH)

If the thought of preparing butterflied fish causes you some anxiety, ask the fishmonger to do it for you when purchasing the fish for this recipe. Alternatively, use two fish fillets to sandwich filling.

Ingredients

Firm white fish	1, whole, about 1 kg (2 lb 3 oz), use snapper or similar
Salt	to taste
Cooking oil	2 Tbsp + enough for shallow-frying
Onion	1, large, peeled and finely diced
Garlic	4 cloves, peeled and finely chopped
Fish curry powder	2 tsp
Coriander leaves (cilantro)	200 g (7 oz), cleaned and finely chopped
Tamarind pulp	200 g (7 oz), mixed with 250 ml (8 fl oz / 1 cup) water and strained for juice

Dry Mixture (combined)

Plain (all-purpose) flour	60 g (2 oz / ½ cup)
Ground turmeric	1 tsp

Step-By-Step

Lightly coat both sides of butterflied fish with combined plain flour and turmeric, then shake off any excess before frying until golden brown on both sides.

With fried fish like an open book, spoon filling onto the side with the tail attached and spread evenly.

Tip: Some Iranian cooks place the stuffed fish, laid on a baking tray and covered with aluminium foil, in a preheated oven at 150°C (300°F) for 20 minutes before serving; this helps the flavours of the fish and filling to further develop and mature.

Method

- Cut off fish head and discard, then cut along the belly and as close as possible to the central bone as though filleting, but do not cut through the fin side; this is to open up the fish butterfly style. Repeat with other side, then carefully remove central bone and discard.
- Wash and drain butterflied fish well, then pat dry using paper towels and season with salt.
- Lightly coat fish on both sides with dry mixture and shake off any excess.

- Shallow-fry fish, opened up, in hot oil until golden brown on both sides. Drain on paper towels and set aside.
- Heat 2 Tbsp oil in a pan. Fry onion over low heat until translucent and lightly browned. Add garlic and curry powder and stir-fry until fragrant.
- Add coriander and sauté for about 15 minutes or until juices from coriander have evaporated and pan is dry.
- Add tamarind juice and salt to taste. Continue to cook, stirring, until thick. Remove from heat.

- Place fried fish on a serving plate like an open book, with insides facing up. Spoon filling onto the side with the tail attached and spread evenly, then fold other side over to cover filling.
- Serve with plain rice (see pg 82) or broad bean rice (see pg 89).

SAFFRON CHICKEN

Iran has long been a world-leading producer of saffron, and given that history, it is no surprise that there is a dish in the country's cuisine that places the treasured spice centre stage and celebrates its unique aroma and flavour.

Ingredients

Chicken	1, small, about 1.2 kg (2 lb 8 oz), skinned
Cooking oil	2 Tbsp
Onion	1, medium, peeled and finely diced
Ground saffron	1 Tbsp, mixed with 4 Tbsp hot water
Tomato paste	1 Tbsp or more to taste
Salt	to taste

Step-By-Step

Cut chicken into 8 pieces symmetrically: first cut off both wings, then both thighs (legs) and quarter remaining body.

After adding chicken pieces, sauté until meat changes colour before pouring saffron solution over. The rich yellow colour of saffron will be immediately visible.

After adding tomato paste and salt to taste, stir to mix ingredients well before adding 250 ml (8 fl oz / 1 cup) water.

Method

- Cut chicken into 8 pieces symmetrically. Wash and drain well, then set aside.
- Heat oil in a stew pan over low heat. Fry onion until translucent and lightly browned.
- Add chicken and fry with onion for about 5 minutes or until meat changes colour.
- Pour saffron solution over chicken, then add tomato paste and salt to taste. Stir to mix well.
- Add 250 ml (8 fl oz / 1 cup) water and continue to cook over low heat for 45 minutes or until chicken is tender. Adjust seasoning to taste, if necessary.
- Serve with plain rice (see pg 82) or flat bread.
- Garnish, if desired, with fried, saffron-infused onions (see pg 16).

Blend (process) whole walnuts until a thick, coarse paste forms, then transfer to a pot.

Simmer ground walnuts in 1 litre (32 fl oz / 4 cups) water for about 2 hours or until a 1-cm (1/2-in) layer of walnut oil has risen to the surface.

Pomegranate concentrate has the pouring consistency of molasses. If unavailable, substitute with tomato paste.

Tip: This dish varies from region to region in Iran. Some cooks prefer sour renditions, while others like it sweet. If pomegranate concentrate is unavailable, substitute with 2 Tbsp tomato paste, but adjust to taste with sugar as it may be too tart.

   Try replacing the chicken in this recipe with duck for variation, and to save time, the walnut paste can be simmered until oily in advance and frozen until needed.

GROUND WALNUT STEW
(KHORESH-E FESENJAN)

Do not be put off by the considerable amount of oil on the surface of this dish as it is neither excessive cooking oil nor oil leached from the chicken. This oil, like olive oil, is a welcome sight because it emerged from the walnuts after prolonged simmering.

Ingredients

Shelled whole walnuts	400 g (13 1/2 oz)
Chicken	1, small, about 1.2 kg (2 lb 8 oz)
Cooking oil	2 Tbsp
Onion	1, medium, peeled and finely diced
Pomegranate concentrate	500 ml (16 fl oz / 2 cups), or 2 Tbsp tomato paste
Salt	to taste
Sugar (optional)	1 Tbsp or more to taste

Method

- Put walnuts in a blender (processor) and blend into a thick, coarse paste. Transfer paste to a pot and add 1 litre (32 fl oz / 4 cups) water. Place over low heat to simmer, stirring occasionally, for about 2 hours or until thickened and a 1-cm (1/2-in) layer of walnut oil has risen to the surface.

- Meanwhile, cut chicken into 8 pieces symmetrically (see pg 45), then wash and drain well.
- Heat oil in a stew pan over medium-low heat and fry onion briefly, then add chicken pieces and fry until they change colour and onions are lightly browned.

- When walnut gravy is thick and oily, add sautéed chicken and pomegranate concentrate or tomato paste. Simmer for about 45 minutes or until chicken is tender.
- Season to taste with salt and sugar, if using tomato paste. Serve warm with plain rice (see pg 82).

When mixing chicken pieces with seasoning ingredients, lightly knead them to help the flavours penetrate the meat.

These flat skewers are as common as tea in Iran, but if unavailable, simply use 2 regular rod skewers in place of a flat one to hold up chicken pieces.

Once chicken is cooked to your liking, remove from heat immediately and allow meat to rest a little before removing from skewers.

SPRING CHICKEN KEBAB
(JOOJEH KABAB)

Kebabs are a favourite food of Iranians, and this one involves tender, juicy chicken with that irresistibly smoky flavour. Iranian-style kebabs are turned frequently during cooking.

Ingredients

Spring chicken	1, whole, about 800 g (1³/₄ lb)
Onion	1, large, peeled and cut into chunks or grated
Ground saffron	2 tsp
Lemon juice	125 ml (4 fl oz / ¹/₂ cup)
Olive oil	2 Tbsp
Salt	to taste
Ground black pepper	to taste

Method

- Cut chicken into 10 pieces symmetrically, discarding backbone. Wash and drain well, then place in a mixing bowl.
- Add all remaining ingredients and mix well, then cover and leave to marinate in the refrigerator, preferably for 3–4 hours before cooking.
- Thread chicken pieces onto skewers and grill (broil) over hot charcoal until they are cooked and charred in parts, but still juicy.
- Serve with flat bread or plain rice (see pg 82).

CHICKEN AND MAYONNAISE SALAD (SALAD OLVIEH)

This salad, a legacy of French influence in pre-revolution Iran, is tastier when eaten the next day, so plan ahead and prepare this dish so that it can be refrigerated overnight.

Ingredients

Chicken breasts	2, about 500 g (1 lb 1½ oz)
Onion	1, medium, peeled and thinly sliced
Ground turmeric	½ tsp
Salt	to taste
Potatoes	2, large, peeled, boiled until tender and grated
Eggs	4, hard-boiled, shelled and grated
Cucumber pickle	150 g (5 oz / 1 cup), diced
Canned green peas	200 g (7 oz / 1 cup), drained
Mayonnaise	4 Tbsp or more to taste

Allow chicken breasts to cool in the stock before draining them to shred. This makes the meat more flavourful.

To hard-boil eggs: place them in a pot, add enough cold water to cover and bring to the boil, then switch off heat and let stand for 10–12 minutes before shelling.

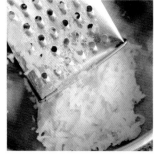

Boil peeled potatoes until tender, then drain and grate when cool enough to handle.

Method

- Put chicken breasts, onion, turmeric and salt in a pot. Add 500 ml (16 fl oz / 2 cups) water and place over low heat. Simmer until chicken is cooked. Remove pot from heat and allow to cool.
- Drain and shred chicken, discarding skins and bones, then place in a large container with a snug-fitting cover.
- Add all remaining ingredients and mix well, then cover and refrigerate until needed.
- Serve chilled with any kind of bread.

Sautéing the split peas in oil for 2–3 minutes before stewing them helps them to keep their shape and not disintegrate during cooking.

After simmering for about 1 hour, the gravy of the stew should be thick and a little oily at the surface. Skim off oil, if preferred.

Do not peel and slice the potatoes long before the stew is ready. This is because they will discolour and turn out darker and less attractive when fried.

S
t
e
p
-
B
y
-
S
t
e
p

SPLIT PEA STEW
(KHORESH-E GHEYMEH)

Attractively golden and appetisingly aromatic, the crown of fried potato strips is suitably inviting for the hearty and delicious stew underneath.

Ingredients

Dried split peas	50 g (2 oz)
Cooking oil	4 Tbsp + enough for deep-frying
Onion	1, medium, peeled and finely diced
Lamb or beef	300 g (10 oz), cut into small chunks
Ground turmeric	1 tsp
Tomato paste	2 Tbsp
Dried limes	3 whole, or juice of 2 fresh limes
Salt	to taste
Potatoes	2, medium

Method

- Wash and drain peas well, then sauté them in 1 Tbsp oil for 2–3 minutes or until they sizzle. Remove from heat and allow to cool.
- Heat 3 Tbsp oil in a pot with a snug-fitting lid. Fry onion over low heat until translucent and lightly browned.
- Add meat, turmeric and fried peas and fry until meat changes colour.

- Mix in tomato paste, cover pot and cook, still over low heat, for 8–10 minutes or until meat is browned. Stir occasionally.
- Add 1.5 litres (48 fl oz / 6 cups) water and simmer for 1 hour or until liquid is reduced to about 500 ml (16 fl oz / 2 cups) and meat is tender. Add dried limes or lime juice and salt to taste, then keep warm over very low heat.

- Peel potatoes and cut into long, thin strips, then deep-fry in hot oil until crisp and golden brown. Drain in a colander, then on paper towels.
- To serve, transfer stew to a serving bowl and arrange fried potato strips in a mound on top. Serve with plain rice (see pg 82).

FRIED AUBERGINE STEW
(KHORESH-E BADEMJAN)

A classic stew that is so loved for its use of aubergines—a favourite vegetable of most Iranians. Like sponges, the pan-fried aubergines absorb the gravy and meat juices while the dish is in the oven and become sensationally flavourful.

Ingredients

Cooking oil	2 Tbsp + as required
Onion	1, medium, peeled and finely diced
Lamb or beef	300 g (10 oz), cut into small chunks
Ground turmeric	1 tsp
Tomato paste	2 Tbsp
Salt	to taste
Aubergines (eggplants/brinjals)	3 large, or 4 medium
Tomato	1, large, quartered
Lime juice (optional)	from 2 limes

Step-By-Step

Fry meat until it changes colour before adding tomato paste and salt to taste. Stir to ensure they are well mixed before adding water.

Peel and slice aubergines while meat is simmering, then pan-fry them until well browned on both sides.

After lining ovenproof dish with fried aubergine slices, spoon fork-tender meat and sauce over to cover completely.

Method

- Heat 2 Tbsp oil in a pot and fry onion over medium-low heat until translucent and lightly browned.
- Add meat and turmeric. Fry until meat changes colour, then add tomato paste and salt to taste. Mix well.
- Add 1.5 litres (48 fl oz / 6 cups) water and simmer for 1 hour or until liquid is reduced to about 500 ml (16 fl oz / 2 cups) and meat is tender. Adjust seasoning to taste, if necessary, at the end of simmering.

- Meanwhile, peel aubergines and cut each one lengthways into 2-cm (1-in) thick slices and pan-fry them in oil until well browned on both sides, then drain on paper towels. Re-oil pan as necessary.
- Line a large, rectangular ovenproof dish with fried aubergine slices, stacking a second layer, if necessary.
- Spoon cooked meat and gravy over and arrange tomato quarters on top. If a more tangy taste is preferred, either add lime juice or use 1 more tomato, quartered.

- Place dish over very low stove-top heat for 30 minutes or in a preheated oven at 150°C (300°F) for 40 minutes; this helps the flavours to develop and mature and allows the ingrediens to heat through.
- Serve with plain rice (see pg 82) or flat bread.

MIXED HERB STEW
(KHORESH-E GHORMEH SABZI)

This is probably the most prepared stew in Iranian restaurants the world over. It is typically robustly herby and quite tart. The degree of sourness, however, can always be adjusted to suit individual tastes.

Ingredients

Cooking oil	4 Tbsp
Onion	1, large, peeled and finely diced
Lamb or beef	300 g (10 oz), cut into small chunks
Fenugreek leaves (*methi*)	50 g (2 oz), cleaned and finely chopped
Ground turmeric	1 tsp
Dried pinto or kidney beans, or black-eyed peas	90 g (3 oz / 1/2 cup), soaked in water overnight and drained
Salt	to taste
Ground dried limes	2 Tbsp, or juice of 3 limes
Dried limes (optional)	4, whole

Greens

Chinese celery	200 g (7 oz)
Chinese chives	200 g (7 oz)
Spinach	200 g (7 oz)

S t e p - B y - S t e p

Soaking dried beans in water for at least 2–3 hours before cooking helps to shorten cooking time considerably. Preferably soak them overnight, so plan ahead.

Instead of chopping by hand, the greens can also be put into a blender (processor), but much of their juices will also be lost.

While meat is simmering, pan-fry chopped greens in 2 Tbsp oil until collapsed and aromatic. This concentrates their flavour.

Method

- Wash and drain greens well, then finely chop them together. Heat 2 Tbsp oil in a pan and fry greens over medium heat, stirring constantly, for about 10 minutes or until they are collapsed, aromatic and darkened. Set aside.
- Heat remaining oil in a clean pot and fry onion over medium-low heat until translucent and lightly browned.
- Add meat, fenugreek and turmeric. Fry until meat changes colour and fenugreek is fragrant, about 8 minutes. Add fried greens and fry for 4–5 minutes more, until well-mixed.
- Add pre-soaked beans and 1.5 litres (48 fl oz / 6 cups) water. Simmer for 1 hour or until liquid is reduced to about 500 ml (16 fl oz / 2 cups) and meat and beans are tender.
- Add salt to taste; ground dried limes or lime juice; and dried limes, if using. Reduce heat to low and simmer for 30 minutes more or until gravy is thickened.
- Adjust seasoning to taste, if necessary, and serve with plain rice (see pg 82).

Peeled potatoes discolour from oxidation if left for more than 10 minutes, so either peel and cut potatoes just before they are needed or soak them in salted water until then.

Unlike potatoes, carrots do not discolour and can be peeled and cut well in advance, then kept aside until needed.

Add carrots and simmer for about 15 minutes before adding potatoes. This is because carrots take longer to become tender.

POTATO AND CARROT STEW
(TAS KABAB)

Utilising the classic combination of potatoes and carrots, this stew is lip-smackingly tasty and nutritious. Serve with flat bread for a simple, hearty meal.

Ingredients

Cooking oil	2 Tbsp
Onion	1, medium, peeled and finely diced
Lamb or beef	300 g (10 oz), cut into small chunks
Ground turmeric	1 tsp
Tomato paste	2 Tbsp
Carrots	2, medium, peeled and cut into 2.5-cm (1-in) thick slices
Potatoes	2, medium, peeled and cut into small chunks
Salt	to taste

Method

- Heat oil in a pot and fry onion over medium-low heat until translucent and lightly browned.
- Add meat and turmeric. Fry until meat changes colour, then add tomato paste and stir to mix well.
- Add 1.5 litres (48 fl oz / 6 cups) water and simmer for 40 minutes or until liquid is reduced by half and meat is tender.
- Add carrots and simmer for 15 minutes or until they are beginning to soften.
- Add potatoes and salt to taste. Simmer for 30 minutes more or until gravy is thickened and potatoes and carrots are tender.
- Serve with plain rice (see pg 82) or flat bread.

When onion is translucent and lightly browned, add meat pieces and continue to fry until they change colour before adding water.

Cut celery into 2-cm (1-in) pieces, then wash and drain well. It is not necessary to discard the leafy tops.

Ground dried limes have a distinct and inimitable flavour, but if unavailable, fresh lime juice is an acceptable substitute.

S t e p - B y - S t e p

CELERY STEW
(KHORESH-E KARAFS)

With the warm, earthy aromas of two types of celery and the zest of mint, this relatively simple stew is an absolute star over plain rice.

Ingredients

Cooking oil	4 Tbsp
Onion	1, medium, peeled and finely diced
Lamb or beef	300 g (10 oz), cut into small cubes
Celery	400 g (13$^{1}/_{2}$ oz), cut into 2-cm (1-in) pieces
Ground dried limes	1 Tbsp, or juice of 2 limes
Salt	to taste

Herbs

Fresh mint leaves	200 g (7 oz)
Chinese celery	200 g (7 oz)

Method

- Heat 2 Tbsp oil in a pot and fry onion over medium-low heat until translucent and lightly browned.
- Add meat and fry for a few minutes or until it changes colour.
- Add 1.5 litres (48 fl oz / 6 cups) water and simmer for 1 hour or until liquid is reduced to about 500 ml (16 fl oz / 2 cups) and meat is tender.

- Meanwhile, wash and drain herbs, then finely chop them together.
- Heat remaining oil in a pan. Lightly fry celery and chopped herbs until softened and aromatic.
- When meat is tender, add fried celery and herbs, ground dried limes or lime juice and salt to taste.

- Reduce heat to low and simmer for 30 minutes or until gravy is thickened.
- Adjust seasoning to taste, if necessary. Serve with plain rice (see pg 82).

CARROT AND PRUNE STEW
(KHORESH-E HAVIJ)

This stew is unusual for its use of prunes or dried plums, which impart a pleasantly mild sweetness and just a hint of tang to the dish. Some cooks are known to add to that sweetness with sugar, while others prefer to emphasise the tartness with lime juice.

Ingredients

Cooking oil	4 Tbsp
Onion	1, medium, peeled and finely diced
Lamb or beef	300 g (10 oz), cut into small cubes
Carrots	500 g (1 lb 1½ oz), peeled if desired and cut into short, thin strips
Prunes	100 g (3½ oz)
Ground saffron	2 tsp, mixed with 2 Tbsp hot water
Salt	to taste
Sugar (optional)	2 tsp
Lime juice (optional)	from 2 limes

Step-By-Step

The saffron solution of 2 tsp ground saffron and 2 Tbsp hot water is merely a guide. Thin it down for a milder taste and colour, or vice versa.

Peel carrots, if desired, and cut them into short, thin strips, approximately 5 x 1-cm (2 x ½-in).

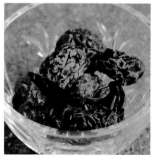

Iranian cooks use one of two main types of prunes—light or dark— for this dish. Shown here are the dark ones (left), while the main image shows the lighter type.

Method

- Heat 2 Tbsp oil in a pot and fry onion over medium-low heat until translucent and lightly browned.
- Add meat and fry for a few minutes or until it changes colour.
- Pour in 1.5 litres (48 fl oz / 6 cups) water and simmer for about 1 hour or until liquid is reduced to about 500 ml (16 fl oz / 2 cups) and meat is tender.

- Meanwhile, lightly pan-fry carrots in remaining oil until just softened, then remove from heat.
- When meat is tender, add carrots, prunes, saffron solution and salt to taste. Stir through, then adjust seasoning to taste with sugar or lime juice, depending on preference.

- Reduce heat to low and simmer for 30 minutes more or until gravy is thickened.
- Serve with plain rice (see pg 82).

Wash kidney beans well, picking over to remove any spoilt ones or debris, then soak them in water overnight.

After straining gravy from meat and beans, transfer them to a container suitable for mashing and keep gravy warm.

Unlike the western potato masher, the Iranian version looks much like a plunger with a solid base (see pg 9), which makes mashing a breeze.

(see pg 9)

S t e p - B y - S t e p

KIDNEY BEAN STEW
(ABGOOSHT-E BOZBASH)

Although the dish is prepared as you would a traditional stew, it is not served as one. The stewed ingredients are drained and mashed together into a thick paste that is served with the gravy and some flat bread on the side. Iranians also call this unique dish *dizi*.

Ingredients

Cooking oil	4 Tbsp
Onion	1, large, peeled and finely diced
Lamb or beef	400 g (13 $\frac{1}{2}$ oz), cut into small chunks
Ground turmeric	1 tsp
Tomato paste	1 Tbsp
Dried kidney beans	150 g (5$\frac{1}{3}$ oz), soaked in water overnight and drained
Potato	1, large, peeled and cut into chunks
Salt	to taste
Dried limes	3, whole, or 1 Tbsp ground dried limes, or juice of 2 limes

Herbs

Chinese celery	200 g (7 oz)
Chinese chives	200 g (7 oz)

Method

- Heat 2 Tbsp oil in a pot and fry onion over medium-low heat until translucent and lightly browned.
- Add meat and turmeric. Fry until meat changes colour, then add tomato paste and stir to mix well.
- Add pre-soaked beans and 2 litres (64 fl oz / 8 cups) water, then simmer for 1 hour or until meat is tender.
- Meanwhile, wash and drain herbs well, then finely chop them together.

- Heat remaining oil in a pan and fry herbs until collapsed, darkened and aromatic. Remove from heat and set aside.
- When meat and beans are tender, add all remaining ingredients, including fried herbs.
- Reduce heat to low and simmer for 30 minutes or until gravy is thickened.
- Strain gravy from solid ingredients and keep warm, then mash solid ingredients into a thick paste.

- Serve paste warm with gravy and flat bread on the side.
- Iranians typically eat the paste wrapped in flat bread. The gravy, which would be divided into individual portions, is consumed somewhat like soup and with more bread, torn into little pieces to soak up the flavourful gravy.

MINCED LAMB KEBABS
(KABAB-E KOOBIDEH)

When served with rice, these kebabs become a meal known as *chelo kabab*, a favourite among Iranians of all ages. The grilled tomatoes are served whole, which diners take from the serving plate to put on their own, where the charred skins are removed and set aside, not eaten.

Ingredients

Minced lamb shoulder	500 g (1 lb 1½ oz)
Onion	1, large, peeled, grated and squeezed of excess juice
Salt	to taste
Ground black pepper	to taste
Flat skewers	3, each about 2.5 cm (1 in) wide and 60 cm (24 in) long
Ground sumac (optional)	to taste
Tomatoes	2–4, medium, depending on taste

Step-By-Step

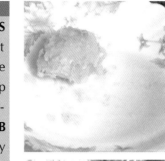

After grating onion, squeeze out its excess juice. Squeezed onion should be moist to the touch but not dripping wet.

After shaping meat onto skewers, use your finger to make marks at 2.5-cm (1-in) intervals, if desired. This creates bite-size portions when the kebabs are cooked.

After grilling, let kebabs rest a while before carefully taking them off the skewers. It is traditionally important to serve them in long pieces.

Tip: These kebabs can be baked in the oven if charcoal heat is unavailable. Shape minced meat into 3-cm (1½-in) wide lengths on an oiled baking tray, then bake in a preheated oven at 180°C (350°F) for 15 minutes on each side.

Method

- Put meat in a mixing bowl. Add onion and season to taste with salt and pepper.
- Mix ingredients together by hand and knead for about 20–30 minutes or until meat feels sticky.
- Take a fistful of meat and, beginning at the pointed end, spread evenly along flat skewer to cover about 30 cm (12 in).
- After shaping meat along skewer, lightly squeeze meat to make sure it sticks to the skewer. Repeat until ingredients are used up.
- Grill (broil) meat over hot charcoal, turning frequently, until it is cooked and charred in parts, but still juicy. Remove from heat and place on a plate to rest.
- Thread tomatoes whole onto regular skewers, then grill them until just softened and their skins are a little charred. Remove from heat.
- Take meat off skewers and place on a serving plate. Sprinkle sumac over and serve with grilled tomatoes and decorated plain rice (see pg 85) or flat bread. Some cooks also add a few sprigs of basil leaves.

After cutting the meat into fillets, lightly pound each one with the spine of a knife or a meat mallet; this helps to tenderise them.

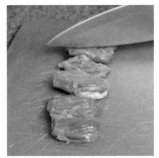

Thread fillets lengthways onto flat skewers, pushing down to crumple them. Use 2 regular skewers for every flat one, if unavailable, to prop up meat.

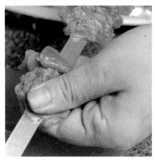

Sprinkle salt on the kebabs only after they are cooked. This is because salt causes the flavourful juices to be leached from the meat and drip away during grilling.

LAMB FILLET KEBABS
(KABAB-E BARG)

Taken from a flavourful part of the animal, the meat here has to be well-tenderised and not overcooked or it will turn out extremely tough.

Ingredients

Lamb loin	500 g (1 lb 1½ oz)
Onions	2, large, peeled and grated
Ground black pepper	to taste
Tomatoes	2–4, medium, depending on taste
Salt	to taste
Ground sumac	to taste
Basil leaves (optional)	a few sprigs

Method

- Cut meat into fillets, each about 6 x 3 cm (2½ x 1½ in) and about 1-cm (½-in) thick.
- Pound each fillet lightly using a meat mallet or the spine of a knife until flattened, then put in a mixing bowl.

- Add onions and pepper to taste. Mix well and leave to marinate for at least 2–3 hours in the refrigerator, covered, until meat is tenderised.
- Thread fillets onto skewers and grill (broil) over hot charcoal, turning frequently, until it is charred in parts but still juicy. Remove from heat.

- Thread tomatoes whole onto regular skewers and grill until they are just softened and their skins are a little charred. Remove from heat.
- Sprinkle desired amounts of salt and sumac over cooked meat and serve with flat bread or plain rice (see pg 82), as well as grilled tomatoes and a few sprigs of basil leaves, if desired.

Mix together all ingredients and refrigerate, covered. The longer the meat is left to marinate, the more tender it becomes.

Thread marinated meat cubes onto regular skewers for grilling.

Iranians typically use a piece of flat bread to hold the cooked lamb cubes when pulling the skewer out.

LAMB CUBE KEBABS
(KABAB-E CHENGEH)

These tender, juicy pieces of lamb, brushed with that inimitable smoky aroma that only charcoal-grilling can impart, are usually served with flat bread. It is rare for anyone to be able to turn away from them.

Ingredients

Lamb	500 g (1 lb 1½ oz), cut into 2.5-cm (1-in) cubes
Onions	2, large, peeled and cut into small chunks
Plain or Greek yoghurt	500 ml (16 fl oz / 2 cups)
Salt	to taste
Ground black pepper	to taste

Method
- Put meat into a mixing bowl and add all remaining ingredients, seasoning to taste with salt and pepper.
- Mix well and refrigerate, covered, for at least 2–3 hours, or preferably overnight, before grilling.
- Thread marinated meat onto skewers and grill (broil) over hot charcoal, turning frequently, until it is cooked and charred in parts, but still juicy.
- Serve with flat bread and, if desired, some basil leaves and grilled tomatoes.

POTATO AND MEAT CUTLETS
(KOTLET)

Iranian meat and potato cutlets differ from those in other cuisines not so much in terms of taste, but how it is eaten—wrapped in flat bread with tomato slices, raw salad leaves or herbs and a squeeze of lime juice.

Ingredients

Potatoes	4, medium
Onion	1, medium, peeled and grated
Garlic	2 cloves, peeled and grated
Minced lamb or beef	200 g (7 oz)
Egg	1
Salt	to taste
Ground black pepper	to taste
Plain (all-purpose) flour	3 Tbsp
Cooking oil	4 Tbsp + as required

Step-By-Step

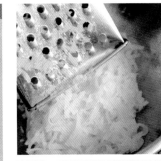

Once boiled potatoes have cooled, peel and grate them into a mixing bowl.

After adding all remaining cutlet ingredients to grated potatoes, mix them together by hand, kneading to mix well and for flavours to infuse.

If the cutlets are breaking up in the pan or sticking to your hands, mix 1–2 tsp flour into the meat and potato mixture before shaping more.

Method

- Boil potatoes, whole and unpeeled, in water until cooked, then drain and allow to cool.
- Peel and grate boiled potatoes into a mixing bowl. Add all remaining ingredients, except flour and oil, and mix well by hand.
- With clean, floured hands, take 1 rounded (heaped) Tbsp mixture and roll it in flour before flattening and shaping into a teardrop or circle. Repeat until ingredients are used up.
- Heat 4 Tbsp oil in a pan over medium heat. Fry cutlets until well-browned on both sides and drain well on paper towels. Re-oil pan as necessary.

CABBAGE ROLLS
(DOLMEH KALAM)

These rolls are sweetish with a slight tang from the vinegar and tomato paste. The filling of meat, herbs, rice and split peas not only tastes great, but also has a lovely variety of textures.

Ingredients

Cabbage	1 head, small
Butter	110 g (4 oz / $\frac{1}{2}$ cup), cut into small cubes
Tomato paste	2 Tbsp, mixed with 4 Tbsp water
Sugar	55 g (2 oz / $\frac{1}{4}$ cup)
Vinegar	4 Tbsp

Filling

Minced beef or lamb	200 g (7 oz)
Onion	1, medium, peeled and grated
Tarragon	100 g (3$\frac{1}{2}$ oz), washed and finely chopped
Basil leaves	50 g (2 oz), washed and finely chopped
Thai fragrant rice	35 g (1 oz), washed and soaked in water for 30 minutes
Dried split peas	95 g (3$\frac{1}{2}$ oz / $\frac{1}{2}$ cup), washed and soaked in water for 30 minutes
Salt	to taste
Ground black pepper	to taste

Step-By-Step

To separate cabbage leaves, first cut around the stump at the bottom, about 5-cm (2-in) deep, then remove. Starting from the hole left behind, pull leaves apart to separate.

Cut away the hard, central stem of each boiled cabbage leaf. It does not matter if the leaves tear, simply double-wrap to prevent leaks.

If the base of the pot is fully covered, and you have more ingredients, stack rolls on top to create a second layer. The inverted plate will hold the rolls in place.

Tip: The same filling can be used to stuff other ingredients such as tomatoes, green capsicums (bell peppers) or aubergines (eggplants/brinjals).

Method

- Separate cabbage leaves and boil in water until translucent and pliable. Drain, cool and trim off central stems.
- Prepare filling. Put all ingredients into a large bowl and mix well by hand.
- Unfurl a cabbage leaf on a clean work surface and put 1 Tbsp filling just below the centre.
- Wrap up tightly: fold lower edge over filling, then fold in left and right sides and roll up.
- Place first cabbage roll in a clean pot. Repeat until ingredients are used up, packing rolls snugly next to each other.
- Sprinkle butter on top and pour tomato paste solution over, then invert a plate and place on top of cabbage rolls, pressing down lightly.
- Add water until plate is half immersed, then cook over very low heat for about 1$\frac{1}{2}$ hours or until all the liquid has been absorbed and filling is cooked.
- Lastly, stir sugar and vinegar into 250 ml (8 fl oz / 1 cup) water and pour over rolls. Allow solution to be fully absorbed, about 30 minutes, before serving.

Put all filling ingredients into a bowl and mix well by hand. The filling can be prepared a day ahead and refrigerated, covered, until needed.

Frozen or preserved leaves need to be handled with great care. If they do tear, however, simply double-wrap to prevent leaks.

After placing inverted plate over grape leaf rolls, add enough water to half immerse the plate.

GRAPE LEAF ROLLS
(DOLMEH BARG-E-MO)

Grape leaves have a distinctive taste and are well-loved in Iran and many of her neighbouring countries. Fresh or frozen grape leaves, or those sold in jars, can be used for this recipe.

Ingredients

Grape leaves	30–40
Butter	110 g (4 oz / $1/2$ cup), cut into small cubes
Sugar (optional)	55 g (2 oz / $1/4$ cup)
Vinegar (optional)	4 Tbsp

Greens

Coriander leaves (cilantro)	50 g (2 oz)
Spring onions (scallions)	50 g (2 oz)
Dill	50 g (2 oz)
Chinese chives	50 g (2 oz)

Filling

Minced lamb or beef	200 g (7 oz)
Onion	1, medium, peeled and grated
Thai fragrant rice	35 g (1 oz), washed and soaked in water for 30 minutes
Dried split peas	95 g ($3^{1}/_{2}$ oz / $1/2$ cup), washed and soaked in water for 30 minutes
Salt	to taste
Ground black pepper	to taste

Method

- If fresh leaves are available, choose only young ones for this dish. Remove stems from leaves, then wash, drain and boil them in plenty of salted water for 2 minutes or until just softened and pliable. Drain and allow to cool before use. If using frozen or preserved leaves, thaw or drain, respectively, before use.
- Wash and drain greens, then finely chop them together and set aside.
- Prepare filling. Put all ingredients into a large bowl and mix well by hand.

- Lay a leaf on a clean work surface and place 1 rounded (heaped) tsp filling just under the centre.
- Wrap up tightly: fold lower edge over filling, then fold in left and right sides and roll up.
- Place roll in a clean pot. Repeat until ingredients are used up, packing rolls snugly next to each other.
- Sprinkle butter on top, then invert a plate and place on top of rolls, pressing down lightly.

- Add water until plate is half immersed, then cook over very low heat for about $1^{1}/_{2}$ hours or until all the water has been absorbed and filling is cooked.
- If a sweet-and-sour taste is preferred, stir sugar and vinegar in 125 ml (4 fl oz / $1/2$ cup) water and pour over cooked rolls. Allow solution to be fully absorbed, about 30 minutes, before serving.

Parboil rice in plenty of water as you would pasta. When rice is half-cooked, drain using a colander.

The rice grains are half-cooked when they are slightly longer and softer, but still too hard to eat.

While parboiled rice is draining, oil a medium non-stick pot and line the bottom with a layer of potato slices, each about 0.5-cm (¼-in) thick.

Tip: Adding 500 ml (16 fl oz / 2 cups) refrigerator-chilled water to the boiling rice makes the grains stretch and become longer. In Iranian cooking, long, separate grains of fluffy rice are desired, while moist, clumpy rice is considered a culinary disaster.

PLAIN RICE, IRANIAN STYLE
(CHELO)

Iranian cooks typically line the bottom of a pot with potato slices when cooking plain rice or rice-based dishes. The potato slices make for a delicious side dish called *tadig*. The underside of the potato slices would have browned and crisped from prolonged direct contact with the pot, while the rice grains above them become light and fluffy.

Ingredients

Basmati rice	600 g (1 lb 5 oz), washed and drained
Salt	4 Tbsp
Cooking oil	4 Tbsp
Potato	1, large, peeled and thinly sliced
Butter	2 Tbsp, melted

Method

- Put rice and salt in a large bowl. Add enough water to cover, stir through and leave to soak for at least 30 minutes.
- Parboil rice: half-fill a large pot with water and bring to a rapid boil. Add drained rice and allow to boil, without stirring, until grains are half-cooked. Drain using a colander and rinse, if desired, to wash away excess salt.

- Pour oil into a medium non-stick pot and swirl to coat bottom evenly, then line with potato slices.
- Spoon rice over the centre of pot, shaking the spoon as you go so rice grains are loosely stacked. Keep spooning rice over the centre until a mound forms inside the pot.
- Light a medium gas hob and place a flame tamer on top. Wrap pot's lid with

clean cloth before covering, then set pot on top of flame tamer. Dry rice out over medium-low heat for 1 hour or until the grains are cooked and fluffy. If without a flame tamer, reduce heat to low.
- Dish out rice and set aside. Carefully lift potato slices and arrange on a serving plate. Pour butter over rice evenly before serving with potato slices.

BARBERRY RICE
(ZERESHK POLO)

This rice dish makes a great alternative to plain rice, especially for dinner parties. The tartness of the barberries, countered with a little sugar, does wonders in whetting the appetite. Traditionally, this dish is served with Saffron Chicken (see pg 45).

Ingredients

Basmati rice	600 g (1 lb 5 oz), washed and drained
Salt	4 Tbsp
Cooking oil	2 Tbsp
Dried barberries or raisins	100 g (3½ oz), rinsed and soaked for 2–3 minutes
Sugar	2 Tbsp
Ground saffron	3 tsp
Potato	1, large, peeled and thinly sliced
Butter	2 Tbsp, melted

Lightly fry barberries with 2 Tbsp sugar and 1 tsp ground saffron until sugar has melted. If barberries are unavailable, substitute with raisins but omit the sugar.

Create a saffron solution by stirring 2 tsp saffron in 2 Tbsp hot water, then mix in 4–5 Tbsp cooked rice to dye the grains a beautiful orangy-yellow.

There are no rules for arranging the dyed rice, so be creative! Without the barberries, this can also be a quick way to decorate plain rice.

Method

- Put rice and salt in a large bowl. Add enough water to cover, stir through and leave to soak for at least 30 minutes.
- Meanwhile, heat oil in a pan over medium-low heat. Fry barberries with sugar and 1 tsp saffron for 1–2 minutes or until sugar has melted. Remove from heat and set aside. If using raisins, do as for barberries but omit sugar.

- Cook rice as described on pg 82: first parboiling, then drying out in a potato-lined pot until light and fluffy.
- Stir remaining saffron in 2 Tbsp hot water, then mix with 4–5 Tbsp cooked rice until evenly dyed and set aside. Transfer remaining rice to a serving plate.

- Spoon dyed rice over plain rice, creating desired patterns, and garnish as desired with barberries.
- Pour butter over rice evenly before serving with potato slices, or *tadig*, on the side.

MIXED HERB RICE WITH FRIED FISH *(SABZI POLO MAHI)*

This dish of aromatic fried fish atop a bed of rice mixed with fresh herbs is a classic *noruz* dish. *Noruz* is the Iranian new year, which falls on the first day of spring.

Ingredients

Basmati rice	600 g (1 lb 5 oz), washed and drained
Salt	4 Tbsp + more to taste
Firm fish steaks or fillets	4–6, total about 1 kg (2 lb 3 oz), use Spanish mackerel, pomfret or similar
Cooking oil	4 Tbsp + enough for shallow-frying
Lime juice	from 2 limes
Potato	1, large, peeled and thinly sliced
Garlic	2 cloves, peeled and coarsely chopped
Butter	2 Tbsp, melted

Herbs

Dill	50 g (2 oz)
Chinese celery	50 g (2 oz)
Coriander leaves (cilantro)	50 g (2 oz)
Chinese chives	50 g (2 oz)

Step-By-Step

After shallow-frying fish steaks or fillets, drain them well on paper towels so excess oil does not drip into the rice later.

Use the side of a chopping knife to crush garlic cloves so that their skins come off easily. Coarsely chop peeled garlic.

After repeatedly spooning rice over the centre of the pot, a mound forms inside. Sprinkle garlic over, then gently place fried fish steaks on the slopes of the mound.

Method

- Put rice and salt in a large bowl. Add enough water to cover, stir through and leave to soak for at least 30 minutes.
- Meanwhile, wash and drain herbs, then finely chop them together.
- Season fish steaks or fillets with salt, then shallow-fry in hot oil until golden brown on both sides. Drain on paper towels, then squeeze lime juice over fried fish.
- Parboil rice as described on pg 82, then mix drained rice with chopped herbs and set aside.

- Pour 4 Tbsp oil into a medium-large non-stick pot and swirl to coat bottom evenly, then line with potato slices.
- Add rice: keep spooning over the centre so a mound forms inside the pot and shake the spoon as you go so grains are loosely stacked. Sprinkle garlic over and arrange fish on the slopes of the mound.
- Wrap pot's lid with clean cloth before covering, then set pot over medium-low heat (with flame tamer) or low heat (without flame tamer) for about 1 hour or until rice is cooked and fluffy.

- Transfer rice to a serving tray, then pour butter over evenly and top with fried fish. Serve immediately with potato slices, or *tadig*, on the side.

BROAD BEAN RICE
(BAGHALY POLO BA GOOSHT)

The broad beans provide not only great nutrition, but also added texture to this dish of dill-infused rice and tender chunks of meat, which can be with or without bone. The flavourful gravy of meat juices on the side is simply a bonus.

Ingredients

Basmati rice	450 g (1 lb), washed and drained
Salt	3 Tbsp + more to taste
Cooking oil	6 Tbsp
Onion	1, large, peeled and finely diced
Lamb or beef on the bone	500 g (1 lb 1½ oz), cut into chunks, or 300 g (10 oz) lamb or beef without bone
Ground saffron	1 tsp
Frozen broad (fava) beans	150 g (5⅓ oz), skins removed and boiled until cooked and tender
Dill	300 g (10 oz), washed, drained and finely chopped
Potato	1, large, peeled and thinly sliced
Butter	2 Tbsp, melted

Remove and discard pale outer skins of frozen broad beans, then rinse them clean and set aside.

Drain parboiled rice and beans using a colander, then mix in dill.

Be gentle when placing meat pieces on the top and slopes of the rice mound. Do not press down on the rice as you want the grains below to be fluffy as well.

Step-By-Step

Tip: Use dried broad beans if the frozen variety is unavailable, but they demand more work. The dried beans need to be pre-soaked, then boiled in water until cooked and tender before they can be added to the rice in this dish.

Method

- Put rice and 2 Tbsp salt in a large bowl. Add enough water to cover, stir through and leave to soak for at least 30 minutes.
- Heat 2 Tbsp oil in a pot. Fry onion over medium-low heat until translucent and lightly browned.
- Add meat and fry until it changes colour, then add saffron and 1.5 litres (48 fl oz / 6 cups) water. Simmer for about 1 hour until liquid is reduced to about 500 ml (16 fl oz / 2 cups) and meat is tender, adding salt to taste.

- Meanwhile, parboil rice as described on pg 82 and add broad beans 2 minutes before rice is to be removed from heat. Drain using a colander and mix in dill, then set aside.
- Pour remaining oil into a medium-large non-stick pot and swirl to coat bottom evenly, then line with potato slices.
- Spoon in half the rice mixture: keep spooning over the centre so a mound forms inside the pot and shake the spoon as you go so rice grains are loosely stacked.

- Arrange meat pieces on the top and slopes of rice mound, then spoon remaining rice over in the same way, maintaining the mound. Reserve gravy.
- Wrap pot's lid with clean cloth before covering, then set pot over medium-low heat (with flame tamer) or low heat (without flame tamer) for 1 hour or until rice is cooked and fluffy.
- Dish out and pour butter over evenly, then serve with re-heated gravy and potato slices, or *tadig*, on the side.

Leave cooked chicken to cool in the stock, then mix both into prepared yoghurt mixture. If desired, debone chicken first.

Cover bottom of pan with a 1-cm (1/2-in) thick layer of yoghurt, then mix in 5 Tbsp rice and spread out evenly. Rice should cover the entire surface in a thin layer.

To serve, cover pan with a large, inverted plate, then turn both plate and pan over. With a few shakes, the rice cake should dislodge and fall onto plate.

Tip: Instead of cooking this dish over the stove, bake it in a preheated oven at 180°C (350°F) for 1 hour for similar results.

Step-By-Step

RICE COOKED WITH YOGHURT AND CHICKEN
(TAH CHIN-E MORGH)

Moulded by the pan in which it is cooked, this rice dish turns out like a cake and the top layer is crisp in texture and wonderfully flavourful because of the browned yoghurt-coated rice.

Ingredients

Basmati rice	600 g (1 lb 5 oz), washed and drained
Salt	2 Tbsp + more to taste
Chicken	1, small, about 1 kg (2 lb 3 oz), cleaned and cut symmetrically into 12 pieces
Onion	1, medium, peeled and finely diced
Plain or Greek yoghurt	300 g (10 oz)
Eggs	3
Ground saffron	2 tsp, mixed with 2 Tbsp hot water
Cooking oil	1 Tbsp

Method

- Put rice and 2 Tbsp salt in a large bowl. Add enough water to cover, stir through and leave to soak for at least 30 minutes.
- Cook chicken and onion in 500 ml (16 fl oz / 2 cups) water over medium heat until liquid is reduced by half and chicken is tender. Remove from heat and allow to cool.
- Meanwhile, beat yoghurt with a spoon until smooth, then stir in eggs, saffron solution and salt to taste.
- Mix cooled chicken and stock into yoghurt mixture, then cover and refrigerate for at least 1 hour.

- Meanwhile, parboil rice as described on pg 82.
- Add oil to a 26–28-cm (10–11-in) non-stick stew pan and swirl to coat bottom evenly. Add just enough yoghurt to form an even layer about 1-cm (1/2-in) thick.
- Add 5 Tbsp rice and mix well with yoghurt, then spread out evenly. Use the back of a spoon to press down on rice.
- Arrange chicken pieces on top and cover with half the rice. Spoon half the remaining yoghurt mixture all over rice and press surface lightly with the back of a spoon.

- Repeat with remaining rice and yoghurt, pressing more firmly on the surface with the back of a spoon to pack in ingredients and even out surface.
- Wrap pan's lid with clean cloth before covering, then set pan over medium-low heat (with flame tamer) or low heat (without flame tamer) for 1 1/2 hours or until rice on top is cooked.
- Remove pan from heat and allow to rest for 15 minutes before turning out: cover pan with an inverted plate, then turn over both plate and pan and rice cake should slide out. Serve immediately.

LENTIL RICE (ADAS POLO)

This tasty and delicious dish is rich with protein from both lentils and meat. Serve with fresh raw salad and some cucumber in yoghurt for a complete meal.

Ingredients

Basmati rice	450 g (1 lb), washed and drained
Salt	2 Tbsp + more to taste
Cooking oil	6 Tbsp
Onion	1, large, peeled and finely diced
Minced lamb or beef	500 g (1 lb 1½ oz)
Ground saffron	1 tsp
Potato	1, large, peeled and thinly sliced
French (Puy) lentils	150 g (5⅓ oz), washed, drained and boiled until tender
Butter	2 Tbsp, melted

Garnishing

Raisins	150 g (5⅓ oz), rinsed and soaked in water for 5 minutes, then sautéed in 1 Tbsp oil for 2 minutes
Saffron-infused fried onions (see pg 16)	

Step-By-Step

Boil lentils in 1 litre (32 fl oz / 4 cups) water for about 20 minutes or until softened, then drain and set aside.

Fry meat with onions, saffron and salt to taste until all the juices have evaporated and mixture is quite dry, then remove and set aside.

When layering rice and lentils in the pot, be mindful to maintain the mound. Do not press down on ingredients.

Method

- Put rice and 2 Tbsp salt in a large bowl. Add enough water to cover, stir through and leave to soak for at least 30 minutes. Parboil rice as described on pg 82.
- Heat 2 Tbsp oil in a pan. Fry onion over medium-low heat until translucent and lightly browned.
- Add meat and fry until thoroughly cooked, adding saffron and salt to taste. When mixture is dry of pan juices but still moist to the touch, remove from heat and set aside.
- Pour remaining oil into a medium-large non-stick pot and swirl to coat bottom evenly, then line with potato slices.
- Spoon in half the rice: keep spooning over the centre so a mound forms inside the pot and shake the spoon as you go so rice grains are loosely stacked.
- Spoon half the lentils over the rice in the same way, maintaining the mound. Repeat with remaining rice, then lentils.
- Wrap pot's lid with clean cloth before covering, then set pot over medium-low heat (with flame tamer) or low heat (without flame tamer) for 1 hour or until rice grains are cooked and fluffy.
- Prepare garnishing in the meantime and set aside.
- When rice is ready, dish out and spoon meat over, then pour butter over evenly. Garnish as desired and serve with potato slices, or *tadig*, on the side.

HERBED RICE WITH CABBAGE AND MEATBALLS
(KALAM POLO SHIRAZI)

This rice dish from the Shiraz region, south of Tehran, is hearty and nutritious and can be a meal in itself. Shiraz was, and still is, an important commercial centre and is the nearest city to the famed ruins of Persepolis.

Ingredients

Basmati rice	450 g (1 lb), washed and drained
Salt	2 Tbsp + more to taste
Cooking oil	6 Tbsp + enough for shallow-frying
Cabbage	200 g (7 oz), cut into small chunks
Lime juice	2 Tbsp
Minced lamb or beef	400 g (13½ oz)
Onion	1, large, peeled and grated
Chickpea flour	1 Tbsp
Potato	1, large, peeled and thinly sliced
Butter	2 Tbsp, melted

Herbs

Dill	50 g (2 oz)
Tarragon	50 g (2 oz)
Basil leaves	50 g (2 oz)

If meatballs are sticking to your hands while shaping them, mix 1–2 Tbsp chickpea flour into the meat mixture before shaping more.

Fry cabbage in oil until softened and lightly browned, then mix in lime juice before switching off heat to dish out.

Arrange meatballs on top of fried cabbage and rice. Stack them if there is not enough room for a single layer, but never push them down forcefully.

Method

- Put rice and 2 Tbsp salt in a large bowl. Add enough water to cover, stir through and leave to soak for at least 30 minutes.
- Meanwhile, wash and drain herbs, then finely chop together and set aside.
- Heat 2 Tbsp oil in a pan and fry cabbage until lightly browned. Mix in lime juice and dish out.
- Put meat and onion in a mixing bowl. Mix well by hand, adding chickpea flour and salt to taste. Shape mixture into small balls, then shallow-fry in hot oil until cooked. Drain on paper towels.

- Parboil rice as described on pg 82, then mix drained rice with chopped herbs and set aside.
- Pour 4 Tbsp oil into a medium-large non-stick pot and swirl to coat bottom evenly, then line with potato slices.
- Add rice: keep spooning over the centre so a mound forms inside the pot and shake the spoon as you go so the grains are loosely stacked.
- Scatter fried cabbage all over the top and slopes of the mound and arrange cooked meatballs on top. Gently stack a second layer of meatballs if there is not enough

room for a single layer, but never push them down forcefully to fit inside the pot because that will cause the rice grains to stick and clump together. Rather, cook the extra meatballs separately or save them for another use.
- Wrap pot's lid with clean cloth before covering, then set pot over medium-low heat (with flame tamer) or low heat (without flame tamer) for 1 hour or until rice is cooked and fluffy.
- Dish out rice and pour butter over evenly before serving with potato slices, or *tadig*, on the side.

Wash and drain French beans, then trim off ends. Remove strings, if desired, but it is not necessary. Cut beans into 2.5-cm (1-in) lengths.

Heat 2 Tbsp oil in a stew pan over medium-low heat and fry finely diced onion until lightly browned and translucent.

Spoon the gravy with beans liberally over the rice; it should cover the mound like a blanket.

Step-By-Step

FRENCH BEAN RICE
(LOOBIA POLO)

The rice in this dish, having absorbed the flavourful gravy of meat juices, tomato paste and saffron, is not only very tasty, but also dyed an inviting, appetising orangy colour.

Ingredients

Basmati rice	450 g (1 lb), washed and drained
Salt	2 Tbsp + more to taste
Cooking oil	6 Tbsp
Onion	1, large, peeled and finely diced
Lamb or beef ribs	500 g (1 lb 1½ oz)
Ground saffron	1 tsp
French breans	200 g (7 oz), ends trimmed and cut into 2.5-cm (1-in) lengths
Tomato paste	2 Tbsp
Potato	1, large, peeled and thinly sliced
Butter	2 Tbsp, melted

Tip: To shorten cooking time, replace ribs with 400 g (13½ oz) minced lamb or beef. To assemble, first divide rice and meat mixture into 2 equal portions each, then spoon into pot, as described, to form a mound of alternating layers.

Method

- Put rice and 2 Tbsp salt in a large bowl. Add enough water to cover, stir through and leave to soak for at least 30 minutes.
- Heat 2 Tbsp oil in a stew pan. Fry onion over medium-low heat until translucent and lightly browned.
- Add ribs and saffron. Fry for 5 minutes or until meat changes colour, then add beans, tomato paste and salt to taste. Stir until well-mixed.
- Pour in 500 ml (24 fl oz / 3 cups) water and simmer for about 1 hour or until liquid is reduced by half and meat is tender, adding salt to taste.

- Meanwhile, parboil rice as described on pg 82.
- Pour remaining oil into a medium-large non-stick pot and swirl to coat bottom evenly, then line with potato slices.
- Spoon in half the rice: keep spooning over the centre so a mound forms inside the pot and shake the spoon as you go so rice grains are loosely stacked.
- Arrange meat pieces on the top and slopes of rice mound, then spoon half the gravy with beans all over.

- Spoon remaining rice, then gravy, over in the same way, maintaining the mound.
- Wrap pot's lid with a clean cloth before covering, then set pot over medium-low heat (with flame tamer) or low heat (without flame tamer) for about 1 hour or until rice is cooked and fluffy.
- Dish out and pour butter over evenly before serving with potato slices, or *tadig*, on the side.

DESSERTS

Make sure that water is boiling rapidly before adding pre-soaked rice.

When rice is partially disintegrated, add milk and stir through.

Ground cumin is intense in aroma and flavour, so use sparingly. Too much and the delicate taste of the rice pudding could be overpowered.

RICE PUDDING *(SHIR BERENJ)*

A traditional dessert, this rice pudding requires some time and effort to prepare, but the result is unexpectedly divine—rich, smooth and comforting.

Ingredients

Thai fragrant rice	75 g (2½ oz), washed, soaked in water for at least 30 minutes and drained
Milk	1 litre (32 fl oz / 4 cups)
Rose water concentrate	1 tsp or to taste
Ground cumin (optional)	1 tsp
Sugar	110 g (4 oz / ½ cup)

Method

- Bring 1 litre (32 fl oz / 4 cups) water to a rapid boil in a pot.
- Add pre-soaked rice and reduce heat to medium-low. Simmer, stirring constantly, for about 30 minutes. Regularly top up with hot water as liquid reduces and continue stirring until rice grains are partially disintegrated.

- Add milk and continue to simmer, still stirring constantly, for 10–20 minutes, until pudding is very thick; the consistency should be between double (heavy) cream and clotted cream. To test, dip a spoon in and remove; the pudding should cling to the back of the spoon.
- Stir in rose water concentrate to taste, then switch off heat.

- Ladle into a serving bowl and garnish as desired with cumin, if using. Serve hot, with sugar on the side for diners to sweeten to their own taste.

SAFFRON RICE PUDDING

(SHOLEH ZARD)

Chopped almonds and pistachios provide some crunch to this silky smooth pudding flavoured by butter, saffron and rose water. It definitely ends the meal on a high note.

Ingredients

Thai fragrant rice	150 g (5 oz), washed, soaked in water for at least 2 hours and drained
Sugar	300 g (10 oz)
Ground saffron	2 tsp, mixed with 2 Tbsp hot water
Butter	55 g (2 oz / ¼ cup)
Rose water concentrate	1 tsp or to taste
Chopped almonds	55 g (2 oz / ¼ cup), soaked in water for 30 minutes

Garnishing

Chopped pistachios	55 g (2 oz / ¼ cup)
Ground cinnamon	1 Tbsp or to taste

Soak chopped almonds in water for about 30 minutes and drain before use.

Simmer rice, stirring constantly, for 20 minutes or until grains are partially disintegrated before adding sugar.

After stirring in the saffron solution, assess the colour and if a richer colour is preferred, make more saffron solution to add to the pudding.

Method

- Bring 1.5 litres (48 fl oz / 6 cups) water to a rapid boil in a pot.
- Add pre-soaked rice and reduce heat to medium-low. Simmer, stirring constantly, for about 20 minutes. Regularly top up with hot water as liquid reduces and continue stirring until rice grains are partially disintegrated.

- Add sugar and continue to stir constantly to prevent sugar from sinking and sticking to the bottom, then burning.
- When sugar has dissolved, add all remaining ingredients and stir through, then cover pot and cook over very low heat for 30 minutes more so flavours can develop and mature. Stir occasionally.

- When pudding is smooth and thick, ladle into a large serving bowl or divide into individual portions. Garnish as desired with chopped pistachios and ground cinnamon and serve immediately.

SAFFRON HALVA

Traditional Iranian halva has a texture similar to fudge and a taste reminiscent of butterscotch. It is also not very sweet, so use more sugar to make a more concentrated syrup, if preferred.

Ingredients

Sugar	225 g (7½ oz / 1 cup)
Ground saffron	2 tsp
Rose water concentrate	1 tsp or to taste
Plain (all-purpose) flour	120 g (4 oz / 1 cup)
Butter	180 g (6 oz), cut into small cubes

Garnishing

Chopped almonds
Chopped pistachios

Simmer sugar in 500 ml (16 fl oz / 2 cups) water until a golden syrup forms, then remove from heat and allow to cool.

After the butter has been incorporated, the result should be like a smooth, soft dough and moist to the touch. If not, work in more butter.

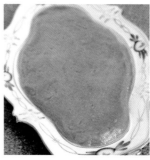

Transfer halva to a flat serving dish while it is still warm and even out the surface with a spatula. If halva cracks at the surface, smooth over with a little cooking oil.

Tip: If for any reason the halva is lumpy or appears like cracked dough at the end of cooking, work in more butter and/or transfer the paste to a blender (processor) and blend until smooth before spreading on serving dish.

Method

- Put sugar in a saucepan. Add 500 ml (16 fl oz / 2 cups) water and bring to a gentle boil, then simmer until a slightly thick golden syrup forms.
- Stir in saffron and rose water concentrate to taste, then remove from heat and allow syrup to cool.
- Put flour in a non-stick pan and place over low heat. Stir constantly until flour is lump-free, light brown and fragrant.
- Add butter, a few cubes at a time, and stir each batch until it is completely melted before adding the next.
- When all the butter has been incorporated into the flour, the result should appear like a smooth, soft dough and be slightly moist to the touch.
- Remove pan from heat and add syrup, stirring to incorporate and until butter oozes out. To test if the halva is ready, drag a spoon over the surface and the trough shape should hold.
- If the halva is not thick enough, return pan to the stove and stir over very low heat for few minutes more.
- Transfer ready halva to a flat serving dish and even out surface with a spatula.
- Garnish with desired amounts of almonds and pistachios and serve.

To double-wrap walnut: first wrap walnut with one date, then use second date to cover exposed part of walnut and press both dates together to seal.

Arrange stuffed dates neatly on a flat serving dish, then set aside to make butter-based topping.

To prepare topping, add butter to browned flour and stir constantly until flour is fully incorporated. The consistency should be syrup-like.

S t e p - B y - S t e p

WALNUT-STUFFED DATES
(RANGINAK)

This easy-to-prepare dessert is a sure-fire hit with family and friends. The sweet and sticky dates offer good contrast against the crunchy and slightly bitter walnuts.

Ingredients

Dried dates	300 g (10 oz), hard tops trimmed off
Plain (all-purpose) flour	120 g (4 oz / 1 cup)
Butter	55 g (2 oz / 1/4 cup), cut into small cubes
Shelled whole walnuts	125 g (4 1/2 oz / 1 cup), halved
Sugar	1 Tbsp
Ground cinnamon	1 Tbsp
Chopped pistachios	1 Tbsp

Method

- Pit dates by gently tearing along their long sides to open up like a book; do not sever into 2 halves.
- With each opened date, put a walnut half where the pit used to be, then wrap up and press to seal, shaping into a large capsule. Double-wrap walnut half if one date cannot enclose it completely.

- Arrange stuffed dates on a flat serving dish and set aside.
- Put flour in a non-stick pan and place over low heat. Stir constantly until flour is light brown and fragrant.
- Add butter and stir until the cubes are melted and incorporated into the flour: the result should be toffee-coloured and

syrup-like in consistency. Adjust with more butter or flour as necessary.
- Pour butter mixture over stuffed walnuts. Sprinkle with sugar, cinnamon and chopped pistachios, then serve.

Choose a wide and flat container for the double cream so that it forms a layer about 1-cm (¹/₂-in) thick when frozen.

Take ready-made ice cream out of the freezer and allow it to thaw until very soft but not completely liquid, about 1 hour.

With melted ice cream in a mixing bowl, quickly take frozen double cream out of the freezer and chop into small chunks to add to ice cream.

SAFFRON ICE CREAM
(BASTANI AKBAR MASHDI)

Traditionally, this dessert was made from scratch, beginning with the ice cream itself, a time-consuming chore. This recipe takes a short cut by way of ready-made vanilla ice cream, but the result is nearly as good. It does require some advance planning as you need to begin preparation at least a day before it is needed.

Ingredients

Double (heavy) cream	250 ml (8 fl oz / 1 cup)
Plain vanilla ice cream	1 litre (32 fl oz / 4 cups) tub, kept frozen
Ground saffron	2 tsp, mixed with 2 Tbsp hot water and cooled completely
Rose water concentrate	1 tsp or to taste
Chopped pistachios	110 g (4 oz / ¹/₂ cup) + extra for garnishing

Method

- Pour double cream into a flat plastic container, cover and place in the freezer overnight.
- The next day, take vanilla ice cream out of the freezer and leave at room temperature for about 1 hour or until very soft but not liquid.
- Transfer melted ice cream to a mixing bowl, then pour in saffron solution and mix well.
- Working quickly, take frozen double cream out of the freezer and cut into small chunks, then mix them into ice cream evenly.
- Add rose water and pistachios and mix well once more, then place in the freezer, covered, until mixture hardens.
- Serve as you would any ice cream and top with a sprinkling of chopped pistachios, if desired.

GLOSSARY & INDEX

GLOSSARY OF INGREDIENTS

Basil
Fresh basil (*Ocimum basilicum*) is frequently served raw alongside Iranian kebabs. The distinctive flavour of basil makes a great foil for the smoky, char-grilled meats, especially when wrapped in flat bread. The herb, part of the mint family, is also used by Iranian cooks in a variety of stews.

Basmati Rice
Iranian cooks around the world favour long-grain rice, and especially basmati rice for that added nutty fragrance. Basmati rice is slightly drier than other varieties when cooked and, in turn, has the added advantage of not clumping together, something Iranian cooks abhor. For the same reason, calrose or glutinous rices are generally avoided. Iranian cooks make an exception only for rice-based desserts, which are prepared with short-grain rice such as Thai fragrant rice.

Chinese Celery
Some Iranians are known to refer to this herb as parsley because of its name in Farsi, so always double-check when exchanging recipes or cooking tips! Chinese celery smells and tastes much like bunched celery stalks, but the latter cannot be used as a substitute for the former in Persian recipes. Celery leaves, while milder, make an acceptable substitute. In Chinese-speaking stores or markets, ask for *qin cai* (Mandarin) or *kun choy* (Cantonese) when shopping for Chinese celery. Malay-speakers know it as *daun sop*.

Chinese Chives

Also known as garlic chives, these flat-leafed shoots have a certain pungency but are definitely not overpowering. Speakers of Mandarin, Hokkien and Cantonese respectively know them as *jiu cai*, *ku cai* or *gow choy*. Although regular chives can be used as a substitute, they lack the bite that Chinese chives impart to the dish.

Dill

Dill is a member of the parsley family and has short, feathery leaves, which Iranian cooks often use in rice or stew dishes. Plain rice is mixed with chopped dill so that it becomes not only aromatic, but also speckled green and very pretty. Dill is also included in herb mixtures that are used to flavour meat-based stews. The herb has a mainly warm aroma with a sour undertone.

Coriander Leaves (Cilantro)

Also known as Chinese parsley, coriander leaves are well loved by the Iranians for their intense flavour. Part of the parsley family, the plant also has edible roots and fruits. The roots are most famously used by the Thais, who grind them into a paste or boil them in a spicy soup. The fruits, when dried, are better known as "coriander seeds", which are used by many cultures around the world as a spice. Coriander seeds are a key ingredient of curry powders.

Dried Barberries

The tanginess of these deep red berries are even more concentrated when they are dried. When preparing *Zereshk Polo* (Barberry Rice), Iranian cooks usually sauté them with a little oil and some sugar to counter the sourness. In Iran, barberries (*Berberis vulgaris*) are believed to have medicinal properties and a variety of food items, such as jam or syrup, are made from them. Barberry juice is also drunk. The Khorasan region in northeastern Iran is the country's largest producer of barberries.

Dried Limes

Typically used in stews, dried limes impart an inimitable tang and musky flavour to the dish. Although lime juice is often cited as a substitute, it pales slightly in comparison to dried limes. Lime juice can achieve the sourness required in a dish but cannot impart that musky flavour, so use dried limes as far as possible. Some recipes call for ground dried limes, which are more similar to lime juice than their whole cousins because its musky flavour, while still present, is also weakened.

Dried Split Peas

Pulses play a prominent role in Iranian cooking and dried split peas, in particular, are best-loved in *Khoresh-e Gheymeh* (Split Pea Stew). The split peas have a pleasant nutty flavour, and unlike beans, they do not take very long to cook.

Dried Roses

Iranian cooks tend to use these as a flavourful garnish. While they can be pungent if you bite into one, the dish is often pleasantly brushed with a faint aroma of roses.

French (Puy) Lentils

These lentils were originally cultivated in the Puy region of France, which explains their names of either French or Puy lentils. Today, other countries such as Italy and the U.S. also grow them. French lentils are favoured over other varieties because of their ability to hold their shape after cooking; other varieties tend to disintegrate. While they also take longer than other lentils to cook, they more than make up for it in terms of flavour.

Grape Leaves

Fresh grape leaves are rare and very much a treat when available. They are best had in spring, when they are freshest and the most tender. Some people have also noted that spring shoots are not yet sprayed with insecticides. Although frozen or preserved leaves are not nearly as delightful, they also make it possible to enjoy *Dolmeh Barg-e Mo* (Grape Leaf Rolls) year-round. Photographed here are the preserved variety that are sold in jars and can be bought from most large supermarkets, although they need to be treated with much care so as not to tear them. Another advantage of using the frozen or preserved ones is that they have already been processed, so that saves you the trouble of parboiling the fresh leaves to soften them.

Japanese Cucumbers

Japanese cucumbers are small and extremely fragrant. Even if eaten with peel and core intact, these cucumbers are still delightful with crunch and with that inimitably fresh cucumber fragrance. Persian cucumbers are similar, if not better, as many Iranians would point out. In fact, so exquisite are Persian cucumbers that they are sometimes treated as fruit and placed alongside other seasonal produce in a large fruit bowl that customarily greets guests to an Iranian home.

Ground Turmeric

This is the rhizome after it has been dried and ground. Just about every Iranian stew has 1 tsp of the spice added when the meat is being sealed (seared). Only small quantities of the spice are ever used, however, because it is strong and can overpower a dish, not to mention dye it an unappetising yellow.

Pickled Cucumbers

These are small Persian cucumbers that have been pickled to be salty and sour. Many Iranian store-bought versions also add that little extra seasoning for variety, with dill being the most common. If unavailable, regular salty dill pickles can be used as a substitute, but adjust the quantity to suit your own taste as different brands are saltier or tarter than others.

Reshteh

These white, dry noodles are brittle and lightly coated in flour. In Iranian cooking, they are most famously used in a thick winter soup called *Ash* (pronounced Awsh). If unavailable, *kishimen*, a type of dry, white and flat Japanese noodles, makes an acceptable substitute.

Pomegranate Concentrate

Pomegranate concentrate is traditionally made by stirring freshly squeezed pomegranate juice over low heat until all the water in it has evaporated and what is left has a consistency that is thick like molasses. The reduction process is very time and labour intensive, however, and Iranian cooks today tend to use the ready-made, bottled variety. The concentrate is used a few tablespoonfuls at a time and imparts to a dish a complex blend of sour and sweet: mainly sour but tinged with a sweetish aftertaste. If unavailable, tomato paste makes an acceptable substitute, but it is also more acidic, so be mindful to add some sugar to counter it.

Saffron Threads

Long dubbed the world's most expensive spice, saffron threads are a prized and key ingredient in Iranian cooking. Unlike other Old World cuisines, however, saffron is rarely, if ever at all, used whole in Iran. Instead, large quantities of saffron threads are ground by hand using a mortar and pestle into powder and stored in airtight containers for future use. That distinctive, appetite-whetting fragrance of saffron becomes more intense when the threads are ground. Iran and Spain rank among the world's top producers of saffron.

Spring Onions (Scallions)

Also known as green onions, these bunches of long, slender leaves are the tops of premature onion bulbs. They are usually used chopped in Iranian and other cuisines and taste mildly of onions. In Iranian cooking, they are usually part of a mixture of herbs that could be stewed or made into a stuffing.

Tamarind Pulp

Iranians generally prefer a tangy taste in their food and this may explain the popularity of tamarind pulp, which has a pleasant blend of sour and sweet. The pulp is usually sold in compressed blocks that also contain a lot of stringy fibres and dark, hard seeds. As a result, tamarind pulp is always stirred in some hot water until it turns a rusty brownish-red in colour before it is passed through a sieve for tamarind juice. In Iran, tamarind pulp is also made into flat, leather-like sheets and eaten as snacks.

Sumac

Dried sumac berries are dark red to brown in colour and, while sometimes sold whole, are typically ground to make a condiment Iranians keep in shakers for their kebab dishes. It has a lip-smacking tangy taste that forms a lovely contrast against smoky, char-grilled kebabs. The plant from which the berries grow can be found throughout the Middle East and in parts of the Mediterranean.

Tomato Paste

Canned tomato paste is a common store-cupboard item in Iranian households and this may have to do with the Iranian love for tanginess. It is often used in small amounts to inject some zest and colour into stews.

INDEX